D1826136

Off-road routes

Back cover photograph: The South Downs Way near Alfriston

First published in 1993 by

Ordnance Survey® and George Philip Ltd, a division of
Romsey Road
Maybush
Southampton
SO16 4GU
Octopus Publishing Group Ltd
2-4 Heron Quays
London
E14 4JP

Text and compilation
Copyright © George Philip Ltd 1995
Maps Copyright © Crown Copyright 1995

Second edition 1995
Fourth impression 1999

Ordnance Survey is a registered trade mark and the OS symbol a trade mark of Ordnance Survey, the national mapping agency of Great Britain.

A catalogue record for this atlas is available from the British Library

ISBN 0-600-58666-9

Printed and bound in Spain by Cayfosa

Acknowledgements
Nick Cotton *back cover, 103, 123, 135* • Reed International Books (Adam Woolfit) *109* • Graham Todd *85* • Andy Williams *24-25, 27, 43, 55, 79*

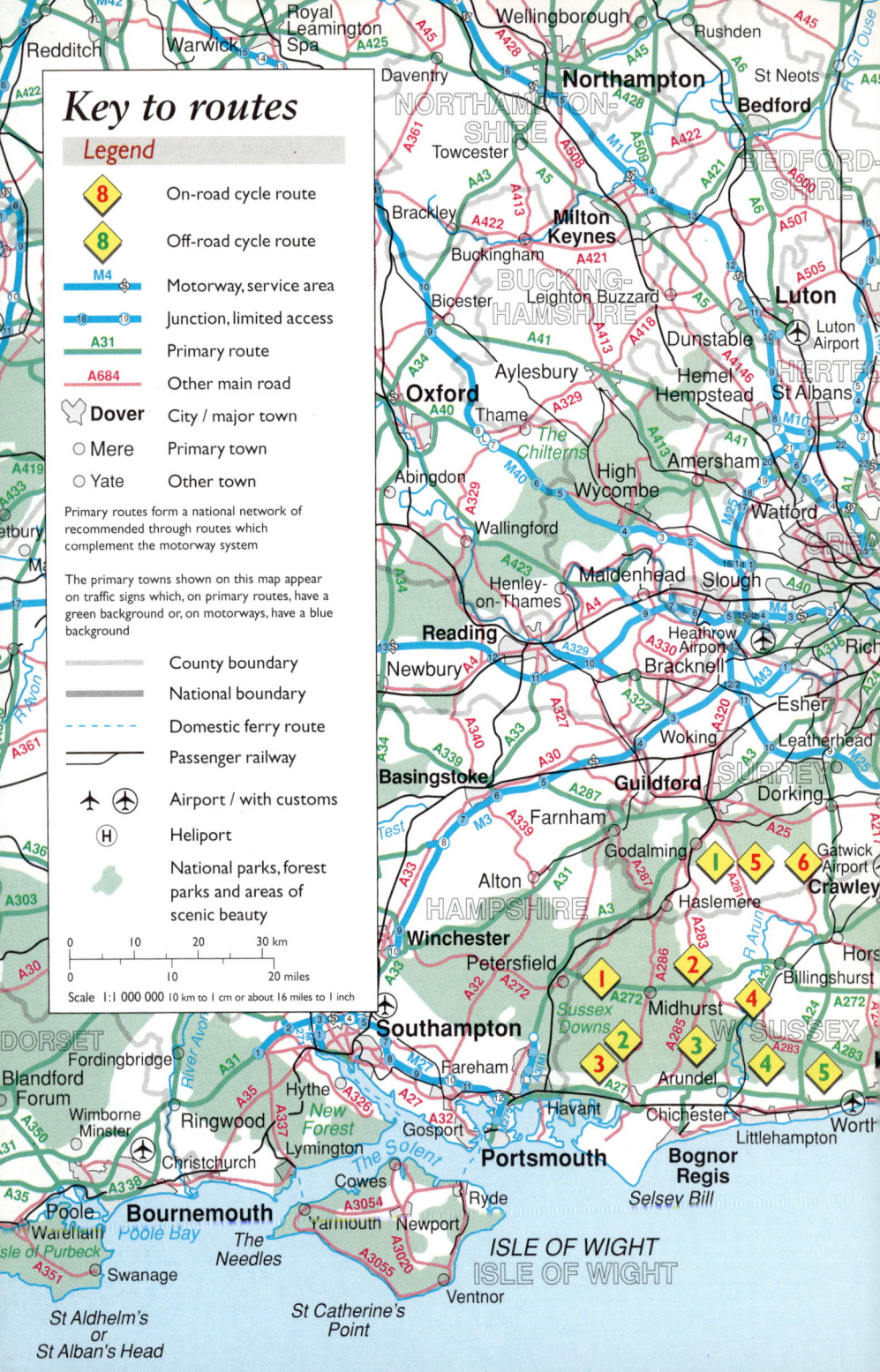

Ordnance Survey

Cycle

24 one-day routes in

Kent, Surrey and Sussex

Compiled by
Nick Cotton

PHILIP'S

TOURS

Contents

On-road routes

Quick reference chart

Route	Page	Distance (miles)	Grade (easy/moderate/strenuous)	Links with other routes [1]	Tourist information centres [2]
On-road routes					
1 Midhurst to Petersfield and back along the foot of the South Downs	18	28	🌿🌿🌿	2,3	Chichester 01243-775888
2 Rolling woodland northeast of Midhurst	24	34	🌿🌿	1,4,5	Chichester 01243-775888
3 Chichester and the South Downs	30	32	🌿🌿	1	Chichester 01243-775888
4 Ruined castles, Roman villas and rough riding west and north of Storrington	36	33	🌿🌿	2	Arundel 01903-882268
5 From Cranleigh through the woods to Gomshall and west to Chiddingfold	42	37	🌿🌿🌿🌿	2, 6	Guildford 01483-444007
6 Quiet lanes, woodland and Leith Hill, east from Cranleigh	48	28	🌿🌿🌿	5	Guildford 01483-444007
7 From Edenbridge via the North Downs to Lingfield	54	33	🌿🌿🌿	8	Sevenoaks 01732-450305
8 East of Edenbridge	60	30	🌿🌿🌿	7	Sevenoaks 01732-450305
9 From Hailsham across the Pevensey Levels and over the Sussex Weald	66	33	🌿🌿🌿🌿		Hailsham 01323-84426
10 Tenterden to Sissinghurst Castle	72	33	🌿🌿	11,12	Tenterden 01580-763572
11 South from Tenterden to Rye	78	33	🌿	10	Tenterden 01580-763572
12 Wye to Chilham	84	32	🌿🌿🌿	10,13	Ashford 01233-629165
13 Narrow lanes and extensive views on the eastern end of the North Downs	90	32	🌿🌿🌿🌿	12,14	Ashford 01233-629165
14 Sandwich and quiet Kent villages in the southeastern corner of England	96	32	🌿	13	Sandwich 01304-613565

Route	Page	Distance (miles)	Grade (easy/moderate/strenuous)	Links with other routes[1]	Tourist information centres[2]

Off-road routes

Route	Page	Distance (miles)	Grade	Links with other routes[1]	Tourist information centres[2]
1 Along the Greensand Way south of Godalming	102	15	🌿🌿		Guildford 01483-444007
2 Glorious downland riding near Goodwood	106	23	🌿🌿🌿🌿	3	Chichester 01243-775888
3 West from Amberley on the South Downs Way over Bignor Hill to East Dean	110	19	🌿🌿🌿🌿	2,4	Arundel 01903-882268
4 East from Amberley over Wepham Down and Rackham Hill	114	15	🌿🌿🌿🌿	3	Arundel 01903-882268
5 North of Worthing: Cissbury Ring to the Adur Valley and Chanctonbury	118	16	🌿🌿🌿🌿		Worthing 01903-210022
6 West from Alfriston over the Downs to Firle Beacon	122	13	🌿🌿🌿🌿	7	Eastbourne 01323-411400
7 East from Alfriston via Friston Forest to Jevington and Windover Hill	126	15	🌿🌿🌿🌿	6	Eastbourne 01323-411400
8 From Wye onto the North Downs to northeast of Ashford	130	16	🌿🌿🌿		Ashford 01233-629165
9 On the North Downs above the Elham Valley, north of Folkestone	134	12	🌿🌿		Folkestone 01303-258594
10 Behind the White Cliffs: the North Downs near Dover	138	16	🌿🌿🌿		Dover 01304-205108

[1]Links with other routes Use this information to create a more strenuous ride or if you are planning to do more than one ride in a day or on a weekend or over a few days. The rides do not necessarily join: there may be a distance of up to three miles between the closest points. Several rides are in pairs, sharing the same starting point, which may be a good place to base yourself for a weekend.

[2]Tourist Information Centres You can contact them for details about accommodation. If they cannot help, there are many books that recommend places to stay. If nothing is listed for the place where you want to stay, try phoning the post office or the pub in the village to see if they can suggest somewhere.

Kent, Surrey and Sussex

The North and South Downs are the dominant geological feature of this region. Shaped like a boat formed by two crescents, the North Downs run from Farnham eastwards to Dover, and the South Downs run eastwards from Petersfield to Eastbourne. Both ranges rise to over 800 feet. In the middle is the Weald, which is, in general, lower and flatter, although there is a hilly area near Ashdown Forest where the land rises to over 700 feet, west of Crowborough. This area is one of the most densley populated in the country but tucked away in the corners of the three counties there are quiet lanes and small villages that are ideal for exploration by bike.

In Kent, 'the garden of England' with its orchards of fruit, there are several areas worth visiting. The eastern end of the North Downs to the north of Ashford has a profusion of tiny lanes and tracks suitable for both on-road and off-road routes; southwest of Ashford, Tenterden is the base for two rides, one of which explores the scenic landscape near Sissinghurst Castle, while the other goes south over the moor of the Isle of Oxney to Rye, one of the Cinque Ports, a charming old town with many attractive buildings.

Moving west, four rides explore the area just to the south of the North Downs. Two start at Edenbridge, one passing Hever Castle and climbing onto Ide Hill, the other climbing onto the ridge of the North Downs. Further west, Cranleigh is the base for discovering the southwest corner of Surrey and the lovely woods around Abinger Common and Leith Hill.

Another cluster of rides is set at the western end of the South Downs, two starting from the handsome town of Midhurst, the others from Storrington and the Roman city of Chichester.

The South Downs themselves are ideal mountain biking country: broad, firm tracks criss-cross the chalk ridges, with their fine views of the Weald to the north and the English Channel to the south. The whole of the South Downs Way has bridleway status and can legitimately be ridden on a mountain bike. Many of the off-road routes described use a part of the South Downs Way to form a circular ride.

Abbreviations and instructions

Instructions are given as concisely as possible to make them easy to follow while you are cycling. Remember to read one or two instructions ahead so that you do not miss a turning. This is most likely to occur when you have to turn off a road on which you have been riding for a fairly long distance and these junctions are marked **Easy to miss** to warn you.

If there appears to be a contradiction between the instructions and what you actually see, always refer to the map. There are many reasons why over the course of a few years instructions will need updating as new roads are built and priorities and signposts change.

If giving instructions for road routes is at times difficult, doing so for off-road routes can often be almost impossible, particularly when the route passes through woodland. With few signposts and buildings by which to orientate yourself, more attention is paid to other features, such as gradient and surface. Most of these routes have been explored between late spring and early autumn and the countryside changes its appearance very dramatically in winter. If in doubt, consult your map and check your compass to see that you are heading in the right direction.

Where I have encountered mud I have mentioned it, but this may change not only from summer to winter but also from dry to wet weather at any time during the year. At times you may have to retrace your steps and find a road alternative.

Some routes have small sections that follow footpaths. The instructions will highlight these sections where you must get off and push your bike. You may only ride on bridleways and by-ways so be careful if you stray from the given routes.

Directions

L	left
LH	left-hand
RH	right-hand
SA	straight ahead or straight across
bear L or R	make less than a 90-degree (right-angle) turn at a fork in the road or track or at a sharp bend so that your course appears to be straight ahead; this is often written as *in effect SA*
sharp L or R turn	is more acute than 90 degrees
sharp R/L back on yourself	an almost U-turn
sharp LH/RH bend	a 90-degree bend
R then L or R	the second turning is visible then immediately L from the first
R then 1st L	the second turning may be some distance from the first; the distance may also be indicated: *R, then after 1 mile L*

Junctions

T-j	T-junction, a junction where you have to give way
X-roads	crossroads, a junction where you may or may not have to give way
offset X-roads	the four roads are not in the form of a perfect cross and you will have to turn left then right, or vice versa, to continue the route

Signs

'Placename 2'	words in quotation marks are those that appear on signposts; the numbers indicate distance in miles unless stated otherwise
NS	not signposted
trig point	a trigonometrical station

Instructions

An example of an easy instruction is:

4 *At the T-j at the end of Smith Road by the White Swan PH R on Brown Street 'Greentown 2, Redville 3'.*

There is more information in this instruction than you would normally need, but things do change: pubs may close down and signs may be replaced, removed or vandalized.

An example of a difficult instruction is:

8 *Shortly after the brow of the hill, soon after passing a telephone box on the right next L (NS).*

As you can see, there is no T-junction to halt you in your tracks, no signpost indicating where the left turn will take you, so you need to have your wits about you in order not to miss the turning.

Fact boxes

The introduction to each route includes a fact box giving useful information:

 Start

This is the suggested start point coinciding with instruction 1 on the map. There is no reason why you should not start at another point if you prefer.

 Distance and grade

The distance is, of course, that from the beginning to the end of the route. If you wish to shorten the ride, however, the maps enable you to do so.

The number of drinks bottles indicates the grade:

Easy

Moderate

Strenuous

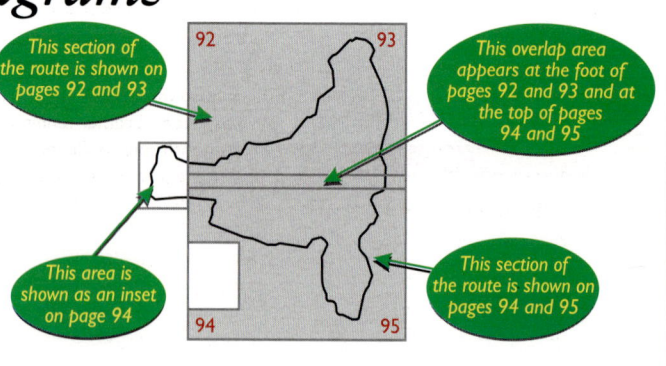

Page diagrams

The on-road routes occupy four pages of mapping each. The page diagrams on the introductory pages show how the map pages have been laid out, how they overlap and if any inset maps have been used.

This section of the route is shown on pages 92 and 93

This overlap area appears at the foot of pages 92 and 93 and at the top of pages 94 and 95

This area is shown as an inset on page 94

This section of the route is shown on pages 94 and 95

92   93
94   95

The grade is based on the amount of climbing involved and, for off-road rides, the roughness of the surface rather than the distance covered.

Remember that conditions may vary dramatically with the weather and seasons, especially along off-road routes

Terrain

This brief description of the terrain may be read in conjunction with the cross-profile diagram at the foot of the page to help you to plan your journey.

Nearest railway

This is the distance to the nearest station from the closest point on the route, not necessarily from the start. Before starting out you should check with British Rail for local restrictions regarding the carrying of bicycles.
(See page 15)

Refreshments

Pubs and teashops on or near the route are listed. The tankard symbols indicate pubs particularly liked by the author.

Before you go

Preparing yourself

Fitness

Cycling uses muscles in a different way from walking or running, so if you are beginning or returning to it after a long absence you will need time to train your muscles and become accustomed to sitting on a saddle for a few hours. Build up your fitness and stamina gradually and make sure you are using a bicycle that is the right size for you and suits your needs.

Equipment

Attach the following items to the bike: bell, pump, light-brackets and lights, lock-holder and lock, rack and panniers or elastic straps for securing things to the rack, map holder. Unless it is the middle of summer and the weather is guaranteed to be fine, you will need to carry extra clothes, particularly a waterproof, with you, and it is well worth investing in a rack for this purpose.

Wearing a small pouch around your waist is the easiest and safest way of carrying small tools and personal equipment. The basics are: Allen keys to fit the various Allen bolts on your bike, chainlink extractor, puncture repair kit, reversible screwdriver (slot and crosshead), small adjustable spanner, spare inner tube, tyre levers (not always necessary with mountain bike tyres), coins and a phonecard for food and telephone calls, compass.

Additional tools for extended touring: bottom bracket extractor, cone spanners, freewheel extractor, headset spanners, lubricant, socket spanner for pedals, spare cables, spoke-key.

Clothing

What you wear when you are cycling should be comfortable, allowing you, and most especially your legs, to move freely. It should also be practical, so that it will keep you warm and dry if and when the weather changes.

Feet You can cycle in just about any sort of footwear, but bear in mind that the chain has oil on it, so do not use your very best shoes. Leather tennis shoes or something similar, with a smooth sole to slip into the pedal and toe clip are probably adequate until you buy specialist cycling shoes, which have stiffer soles and are sometimes designed for use with specialist pedals.

Legs Cycling shorts or padded cycling underwear worn under everyday clothing make long rides much more comfortable. Avoid tight, non-stretch trousers, which are very uncomfortable for cycling and will sap your energy, as they restrict the movement of your legs; baggy tracksuit bottoms, which can get caught in the chain and will sag around your ankles if they get wet. Almost anything else will do, though a pair of stretch leggings is probably best.

Upper body What you wear should be long enough to cover your lower back when you are leaning forward and, ideally, should have zips or buttons that you can adjust to regulate your temperature. Several thin layers are better than one thick layer.

Head A helmet may protect your head in a fall.

Wet weather If you get soaked to your skin and you are tired, your body core temperature can drop very quickly when you are cycling. A waterproof, windproof top is essential if it looks like rain. A dustbin bag would be better than nothing but obviously a breathable waterproof material is best.

Cold weather Your extremities suffer far more when you are cycling than when you are walking in similar conditions. A hat that covers your ears, a scarf around your neck, a pair of warm gloves and a thermal top and bottom combined with what you would normally wear cycling should cover almost all conditions.

Night and poor light Wearing light-coloured clothes or reflective strips is almost as important as having lights on your bike. Reflective bands worn around the ankles are particularly effective in making you visible to motorists.

Preparing your bicycle

You may not be a bicycle maintenance expert, but you should make sure that your bike is roadworthy before you begin a ride.

If you are planning to ride in soft, off-road conditions, fit fat, knobbly tyres. If you are using the bike around town or on a road route, fit narrower, smoother tyres.

Check the tyres for punctures or damage and repair or replace if necessary or if you are in any doubt. Keep tyres inflated hard (recommended pressures are on the side wall of the tyre) for mainly on-road riding. You do not need to inflate tyres as hard for off-road use; slightly softer tyres give some cushioning and get better traction in muddy conditions.

Ensure that the brakes work efficiently. Replace worn cables and brake blocks.

The bike should glide along silently. Tighten and adjust any part that is loose or rubbing against a moving part. Using a good-quality bike oil lubricate the hubs, bottom bracket, pedals where they join the cranks, chain and gear-changing mechanism from both sides. If the bike still makes grating noises, replace the bearings.

Adjust the saddle properly. You can raise or lower it, move it forwards or backwards or tilt it up or down. The saddle height should ensure that your legs are working efficiently: too low and your knees will ache; too high and your hips will be rocking in order for your feet to reach the pedals.

Some women find the average bike saddle uncomfortable because the female pelvis is a different shape from the male pelvis and needs a broader saddle for support. Some manufacturers make saddles especially for women.

Cross-profiles

The introduction to each route includes a cross-profile diagram. The vertical scale is the same on each diagram but the horizontal scale varies according to the length of the route

On-road route

Off-road route

Corfe Castle

Start / finish

Blashenwell Farm

Kingston

Swyre Head

Kimmeridge

Tips for touring

The law

England and Wales have 120 000 miles of rights of way, but under the Wildlife and Countryside Act of 1968 you are allowed to cycle on only about 10 percent of them, namely on bridleways, by-ways open to all traffic (BOATS) and roads used as public paths (RUPPS).

The other 90 percent of rights of way are footpaths, where you may walk and usually push your bike, but not ride it. Local bylaws sometimes prohibit the pushing of bicycles along footpaths and although all the paths in this book have been checked, bylaws do sometimes change.

- You are not allowed to ride where there is no right of way. If you lose the route and find yourself in conflict with a landowner, stay calm and courteous, make a note of exactly where you are and then contact the Rights of Way Department of the local authority. It has copies of definitive maps and will take up the matter on your behalf if you are in the right.

- For further information on cycling and the law contact the Cyclists Touring Club (CTC) whose address can be found on the inside back cover.

Cycling techniques

If you are not used to cycling more than a few miles at a stretch, you may find initially that touring is tiring. There are ways of conserving your energy, however:

- Do not struggle in a difficult gear if you have an easier one. Let the gears help you up the hills. No matter how many gears a bike has, however, ultimately it is leg power that you need to get you up a hill. You may decide to get off and walk uphill with your bike to rest your muscles.

- You can save a lot of energy on the road by following close behind a stronger rider in his or her slipstream, but do not try this offroad. All the routes are circular, so you can start at any point and follow the instructions until you return to it. This is useful when there is a strong wind, as you can alter the route to go into the wind at the start of the ride, when you are fresh, and have the wind behind you on the return, when you are more tired.

- The main difference in technique between on-road and off-road cycling lies in getting your weight balanced correctly. When going down steep off-road sections, lower the saddle, keep the pedals level, stand up out of the saddle to let your legs absorb the bumps and keep your weight over the rear wheel. Control is paramount: keep your eyes on what lies ahead.

Steeple Hill

Grange Arch

Ridgeway Hill

Knowle Hill

Start / finish

Traffic

The rides in this book are designed to minimize time spent on busy roads, but you will inevitably encounter some traffic. The most effective way to avoid an accident with a motor vehicle is to be highly aware of what is going on around you and to ensure that other road users are aware of you.

- Ride confidently.
- Indicate clearly to other road users what you intend to do, particularly when turning right. Look behind you, wait for a gap in the traffic, indicate, then turn. If you have to turn right off a busy road or on a difficult bend, pull in and wait for a gap in the traffic or go past the turning to a point where you have a clear view of the traffic in both directions, then cross and return to the turning.
- Use your lights and wear reflective clothing at night and in poor light.
- Do not ride two-abreast if there is a vehicle behind you. Let it pass. If it cannot easily overtake you because the road is narrow, look for a passing place or a gate entrance and pull in to let it pass.

Maintenance

Mountain bikes are generally stronger than road bikes, but any bike can suffer. To prevent damage as far as possible:

- Watch out for holes and obstacles.
- Clean off mud and lubricate moving parts regularly.
- Replace worn parts, particularly brake blocks.

Riders also need maintenance:

- Eat before you get hungry, drink before you get thirsty. Dried fruit, nuts and chocolate take up little space and provide lots of energy.

- Carry a water bottle and keep it filled, especially on hot days. Tea, water and well-diluted soft drinks are the best thirst-quenchers.

Breakdowns

The most likely breakdown to occur is a puncture.

- Always carry a pump.
- Take a spare inner tube so that you can leave the puncture repair until later.
- Make sure you know how to remove a wheel. This may require an adjustable spanner or, in many cases, no tool at all, as many bikes now have wheels with quick-release skewers that can be loosened by hand.

Security

Where you park your bike, what you lock it with and what you lock it to are important in protecting it from being stolen.

- Buy the best lock you can afford.
- Lock your bike to something immovable in a well-lit public place.
- Locking two bikes together is better than locking them individually.
- Use a chain with a lock to secure the wheels and saddle to the frame. Keep a note of the frame number and other details, and insure, photograph and code the bike.

Lost and Found

The detailed instructions and the Ordnance Survey mapping in this book minimize the chances of getting lost. However, if you do lose your way:

- Ask someone for directions.
- Retrace the route back to the last point where you knew where you were.
- Use the map to rejoin the route at a point further ahead.

Code of Conduct

- Enjoy the countryside and respect its life and work
- Only ride where you know you have a legal right
- Always yield to horses and pedestrians
- Take all litter with you
- Don't get annoyed with anyone; it never solves any problems
- Guard against all risk of fire
- Fasten all gates
- Keep your dogs under close control
- Keep to public paths across farmland
- Use gates and stiles to cross fences, hedges and walls
- Avoid livestock, crops and machinery or, if not possible, keep contact to a minimum
- Help keep all water clean
- Protect wildlife, plants and trees
- Take special care on country roads
- Make no unnecessary noise

Transporting your bike

There are three ways of getting you and your bike to the start of a ride:

Cycle to the start or to a point along a route near your home.

Take the train. Always check in advance that you can take the bike on the train. Some trains allow only up to two bikes and you may need to make a reservation and pay a flat fee however long the journey. Always label your bike showing your name and destination station.

Travel by motor vehicle. You can carry the bikes:

- Inside the vehicle. With the advent of quick release mechanisms on both wheels and the seatpost, which allow a quick dismantling of the bike, it is possible to fit a bike in even quite small cars. It is unwise to stack one bike on top of another unless you have a thick blanket separating them to prevent scratching or worse damage. If you are standing them up in a van, make sure they are secured so they cannot slide around.

- On top of the vehicle. The advantages of this method are that the bikes are completely out of the way and are not resting against each other, you can get at the boot or hatch easily and the bikes do not obscure the number plate or rear lights and indicators. The disadvantages are that you use up more fuel, the car can feel uncomfortable in a crosswind and you have to be reasonably tall and strong to get the bikes on and off the roof.

- On a rack that attaches to the rear of the vehicle. The advantages are that the rack is easily and quickly assembled and disassembled, fuel consumption is better and anyone can lift the bikes on and off. The disadvantages are that you will need to invest in a separate board carrying the number plate and rear lights if they are obstructed by the bikes, you cannot easily get to the boot or hatch once the bikes have been loaded and secured, and the bikes are resting against each other so you must take care that they don't scrape off paint or damage delicate parts.

- Whichever way you carry the bikes on the outside of the vehicle, ensure that you regularly check that they are secure and that straps and fixings that hold them in place have not come loose. If you are leaving the bikes for any length of time, be sure they are secure against theft; if nothing else lock them to each other.

Legend to 1:50 000 maps

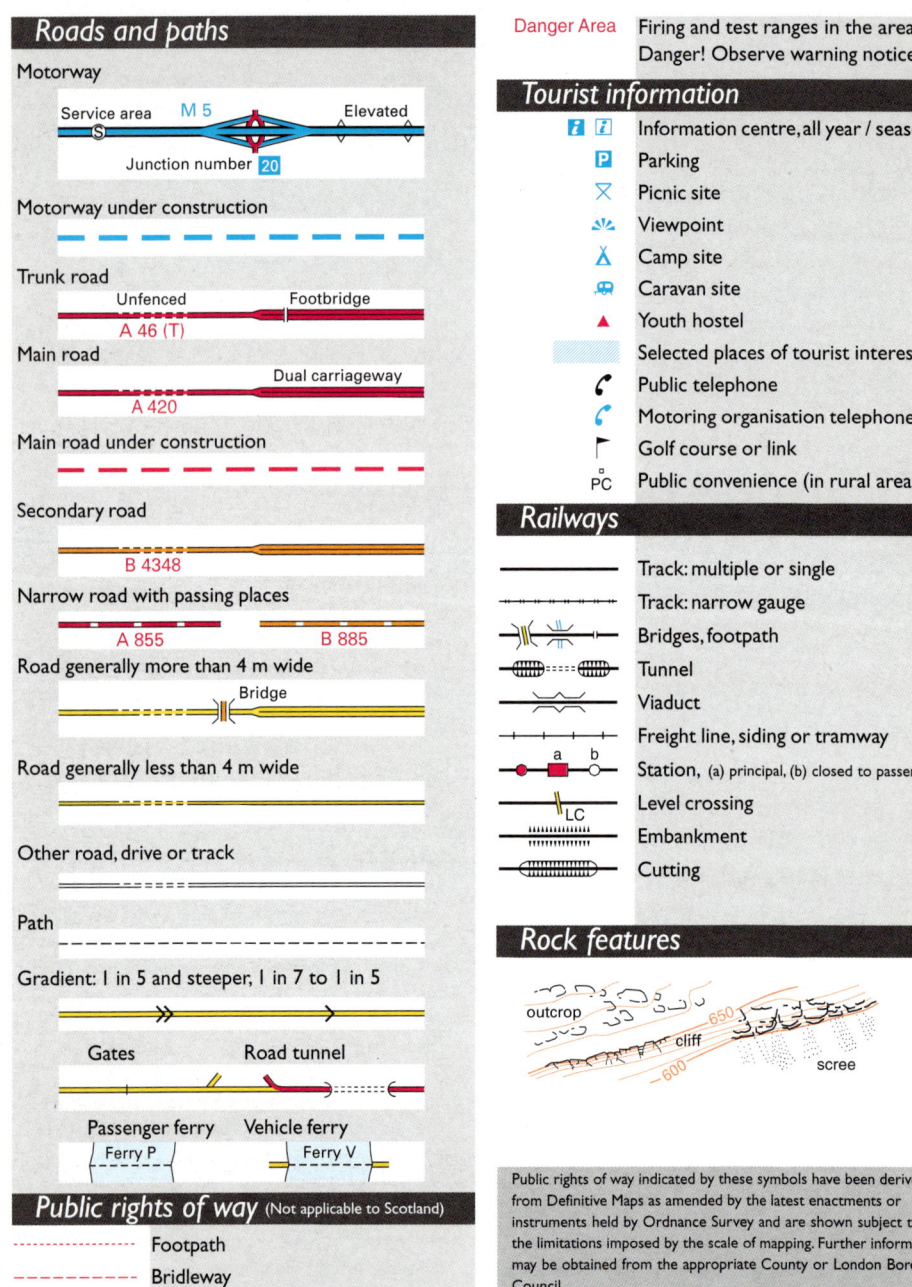

Roads and paths

Motorway

Service area   M 5   Elevated
S
Junction number 20

Motorway under construction

Trunk road

Unfenced   Footbridge
A 46 (T)

Main road

Dual carriageway
A 420

Main road under construction

Secondary road

B 4348

Narrow road with passing places

A 855   B 885

Road generally more than 4 m wide

Bridge

Road generally less than 4 m wide

Other road, drive or track

Path

Gradient: 1 in 5 and steeper, 1 in 7 to 1 in 5

Gates   Road tunnel

Passenger ferry   Vehicle ferry
Ferry P   Ferry V

Public rights of way (Not applicable to Scotland)

- - - - - - - - - - - Footpath
- - - - - - - - - Bridleway
- · - · - · - · - Road used as a public path
-+-+-+-+-+- Byway open to all traffic

Danger Area   Firing and test ranges in the area. Danger! Observe warning notices

Tourist information

ℹ️ ℹ️		Information centre, all year / seasonal
P		Parking
✕		Picnic site
☀️		Viewpoint
Å		Camp site
🚐		Caravan site
▲		Youth hostel
		Selected places of tourist interest
✆		Public telephone
✆		Motoring organisation telephone
⌐		Golf course or link
PC		Public convenience (in rural areas)

Railways

Track: multiple or single
Track: narrow gauge
Bridges, footpath
Tunnel
Viaduct
Freight line, siding or tramway
a   b
Station, (a) principal, (b) closed to passengers
Level crossing   LC
Embankment
Cutting

Rock features

outcrop   650
cliff   600
scree

Public rights of way indicated by these symbols have been derived from Definitive Maps as amended by the latest enactments or instruments held by Ordnance Survey and are shown subject to the limitations imposed by the scale of mapping. Further information may be obtained from the appropriate County or London Borough Council

The representation on this map of any other road, track or path is no evidence of the existence of a right of way

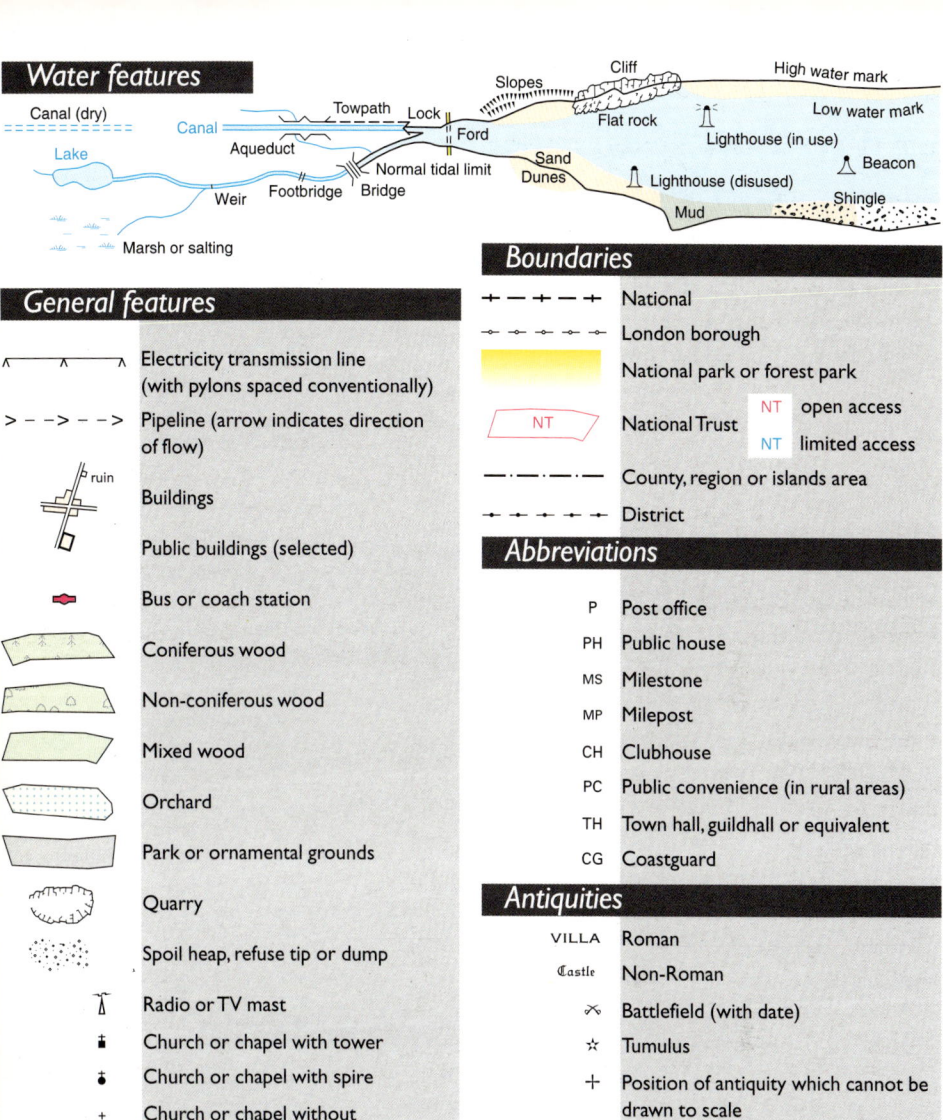

Water features

Canal (dry)

Canal

Lake

Weir

Footbridge

Towpath   Lock

Aqueduct

Ford

Bridge   Normal tidal limit

Marsh or salting

Slopes   Cliff   High water mark

Flat rock   Low water mark

Lighthouse (in use)

Sand   Beacon

Dunes   Lighthouse (disused)

Mud   Shingle

General features

Electricity transmission line
(with pylons spaced conventionally)

> – –> – –>   Pipeline (arrow indicates direction
of flow)

ruin   Buildings

Public buildings (selected)

Bus or coach station

Coniferous wood

Non-coniferous wood

Mixed wood

Orchard

Park or ornamental grounds

Quarry

Spoil heap, refuse tip or dump

Radio or TV mast

Church or chapel with tower

Church or chapel with spire

Church or chapel without
tower or spire

Chimney or tower

Glasshouse

Graticule intersection at 5' intervals

Heliport

Triangulation pillar

Windmill with or without sails

Windpump

Boundaries

+ – + – +   National

London borough

National park or forest park

NT   National Trust   NT   open access

NT   limited access

County, region or islands area

District

Abbreviations

P   Post office

PH   Public house

MS   Milestone

MP   Milepost

CH   Clubhouse

PC   Public convenience (in rural areas)

TH   Town hall, guildhall or equivalent

CG   Coastguard

Antiquities

VILLA   Roman

Castle   Non-Roman

Battlefield (with date)

☆   Tumulus

+   Position of antiquity which cannot be
drawn to scale

Ancient monuments and historic
buildings in the care of the Secretaries
of State for the Environment, for
Scotland and for Wales and that are
open to the public

Heights

50   Contours are at 10 metres vertical
interval

·144   Heights are to the nearest metre
above mean sea level

Heights shown close to a triangulation pillar refer to the station height
at ground level and not necessarily to the summit

Midhurst to Petersfield and back along the foot of the South Downs

Start

The Silver Shoe PH, High St, Midhurst

 Heading north out of town on the A286

Distance and grade

28 miles

 Moderate

Terrain

Three climbs: 300 feet between Midhurst and Milland, 300 feet from Milland to Hill Brow on the A3, 260 feet from Liss to Bushy Hill. Flat from Petersfield back to Midhurst

Nearest railway

Petersfield

The route leaves the valley of the River Rother, taking some impressive sunken lanes through woods north to Milland. It is worth stopping there to look at the beautiful work produced by The Living Tree, including wooden toys from all

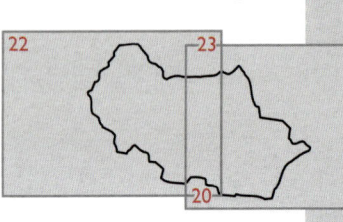

over the world. The ride climbs to cross the A3 at Hill Brow and sweeps down through Liss to come around the back of Petersfield. Around the large square in Petersfield there are many watering holes and attractive Georgian houses. Having left the B2146 at Nursted, the ride is an absolute dream of quiet flat lanes beneath the folds of the South Downs back to Midhurst.

Refreshments

Spread Eagle PH 🍴🍴, lots of choice, **Midhurst**
Rising Sun PH, **Milland**
Crossing Gate PH, **Liss**
Drovers PH, **Hill Brow**
Cricketers PH 🍴, Harrow PH 🍴🍴, **Steep**
Lots of choice in **Petersfield**
White Hart PH 🍴, The Ship PH, Coach and Horses PH 🍴, **South Harting**
Three Horseshoes PH 🍴🍴, **Elsted**

Midhurst　　Woolbeding　　Robins　Milland　　Hill Brow　　Liss　　Bushy Hill

Midhurst (1)

The origins of this town lie in the early Middle Ages when the Norman Lord, Savaric Fitzcane, built a castle on St Anne's Hill. This castle is now completely ruined but there are many other buildings which display Midhurst's history.

Midhurst Parish Church

This church and its beautiful churchyard overlook the Market Square

Market Hall, Town Hall and The Spread Eagle

The timber building in front of the Spread Eagle is the 16th-century Market Hall where the Grammar School was founded in 1672. The Town Hall dates from the early 19th century and still has the stocks and lock up. The Spread Eagle is one of the most impressive buildings in the town.

Petersfield (16)

Once an important town for the wool trade, Petersfield is now a busy market town. A statue of William III guards the central square and there is a large lake southeast of the town.

Petersfield   Nursted   Quebec   Elsted   Treyford   Bepton

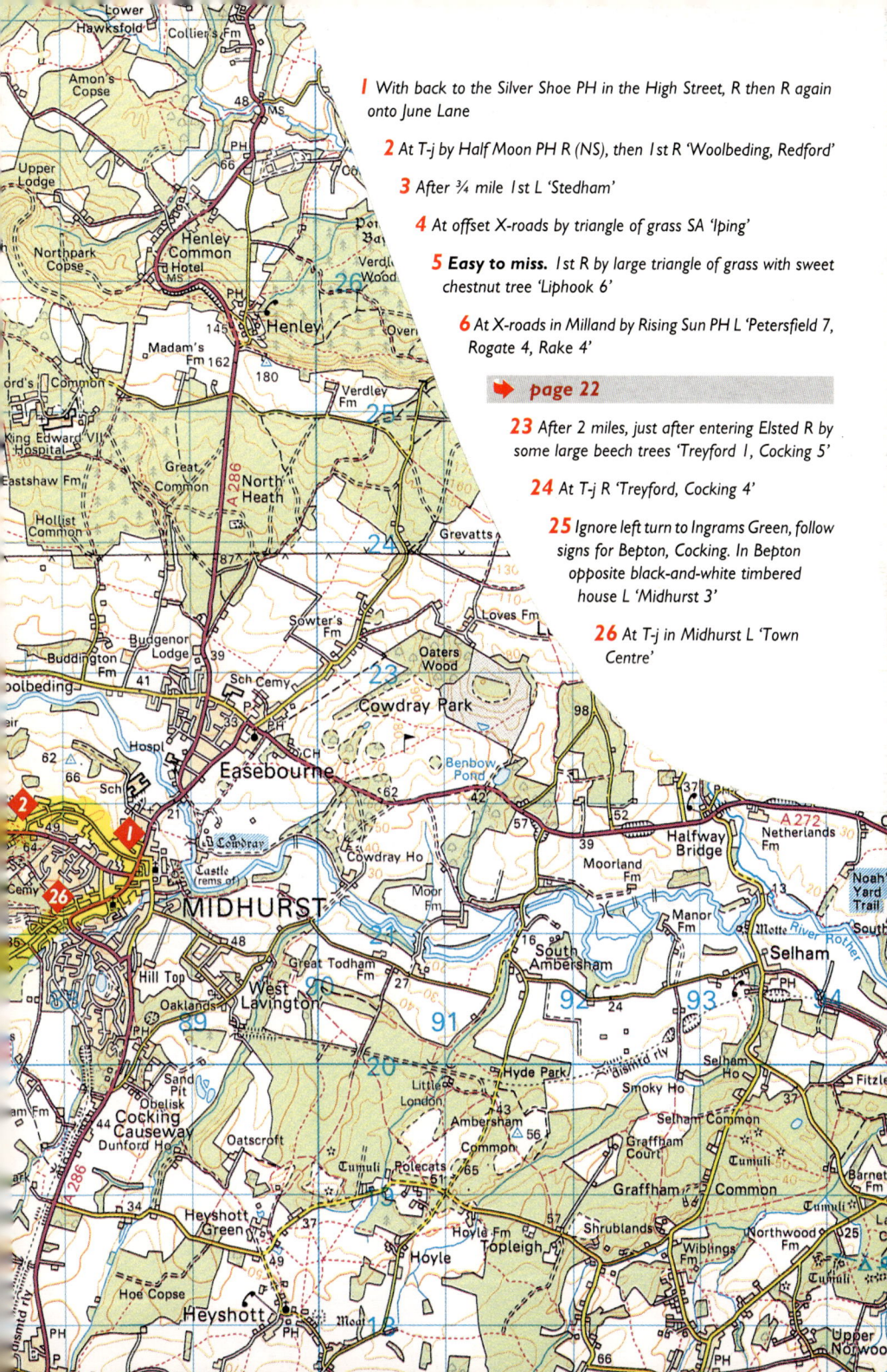

1 With back to the Silver Shoe PH in the High Street, R then R again onto June Lane

2 At T-j by Half Moon PH R (NS), then 1st R 'Woolbeding, Redford'

3 After ¾ mile 1st L 'Stedham'

4 At offset X-roads by triangle of grass SA 'Iping'

5 **Easy to miss.** 1st R by large triangle of grass with sweet chestnut tree 'Liphook 6'

6 At X-roads in Milland by Rising Sun PH L 'Petersfield 7, Rogate 4, Rake 4'

➡ **page 22**

23 After 2 miles, just after entering Elsted R by some large beech trees 'Treyford 1, Cocking 5'

24 At T-j R 'Treyford, Cocking 4'

25 Ignore left turn to Ingrams Green, follow signs for Bepton, Cocking. In Bepton opposite black-and-white timbered house L 'Midhurst 3'

26 At T-j in Midhurst L 'Town Centre'

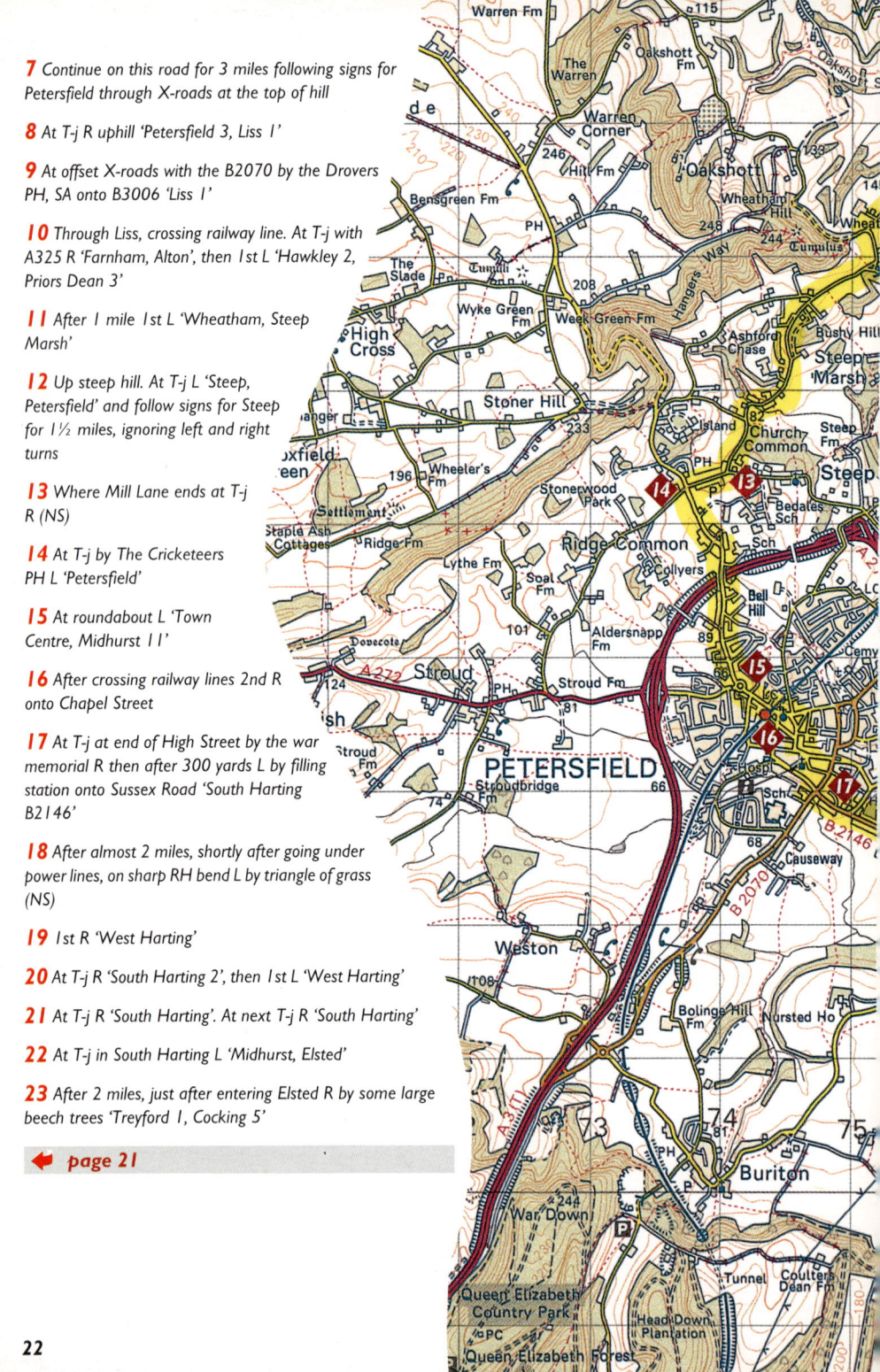

7 Continue on this road for 3 miles following signs for Petersfield through X-roads at the top of hill

8 At T-j R uphill 'Petersfield 3, Liss 1'

9 At offset X-roads with the B2070 by the Drovers PH, SA onto B3006 'Liss 1'

10 Through Liss, crossing railway line. At T-j with A325 R 'Farnham, Alton', then 1st L 'Hawkley 2, Priors Dean 3'

11 After 1 mile 1st L 'Wheatham, Steep Marsh'

12 Up steep hill. At T-j L 'Steep, Petersfield' and follow signs for Steep for 1½ miles, ignoring left and right turns

13 Where Mill Lane ends at T-j R (NS)

14 At T-j by The Cricketeers PH L 'Petersfield'

15 At roundabout L 'Town Centre, Midhurst 11'

16 After crossing railway lines 2nd R onto Chapel Street

17 At T-j at end of High Street by the war memorial R then after 300 yards L by filling station onto Sussex Road 'South Harting B2146'

18 After almost 2 miles, shortly after going under power lines, on sharp RH bend L by triangle of grass (NS)

19 1st R 'West Harting'

20 At T-j R 'South Harting 2', then 1st L 'West Harting'

21 At T-j R 'South Harting'. At next T-j R 'South Harting'

22 At T-j in South Harting L 'Midhurst, Elsted'

23 After 2 miles, just after entering Elsted R by some large beech trees 'Treyford 1, Cocking 5'

← **page 21**

2

Rolling woodland northeast of Midhurst

There is easy cycling on quiet lanes north of the South Downs. This ride links the historic towns of Midhurst and Petworth via a loop through wooded lanes and small villages such as Lodsworth and Plaistow. There are many good pubs along the way and the chance of a tea stop in Petworth or back at Midhurst.

 Refreshments

Plenty of choice in **Midhurst** and **Petworth**
Three Moles PH, **Selham**
Stag Inn, **Balls Cross** Sun Inn, **Plaistow**
Lickfold Inn, **Lickfold**

Background picture: Petworth Park

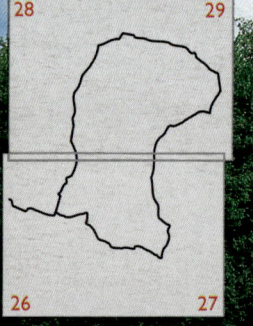

 Start

Knockhundred Road, by the building society in the centre of Midhurst

P Free long-term parking on the A286 Haslemere Road, going north out of Midhurst

 Distance and grade

34 miles
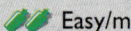 Easy/moderate

 Terrain

In general, flat or undulating, but with two hills of 250 feet in the first half of the ride, one from South Ambersham to the top of Leggatt Hill and one from Lickfold onto Shopp Hill

Nearest railway

Haslemere, 3 miles from the route at Gospel Green, or Billingshurst, 6 miles from the route at Kirdford

Midhurst South Ambersham Lodsworth Lickfold Dial Green Shopp Hill Gospel Green Plaistow

Cowdray House (2-3)

Originally known as La Coudraye, this house was the residence of the de Bohun family when they left the castle at Midhurst. Construction began in 1530 and, despite a fire in 1793 which left the house a standing ruin, it is an impressive example of Tudor architecture.

Lodsworth (6) and Lickfold (7-8)

These villages are typical of the area and are surrounded and bounded by streams and woods. Lodsworth has a charming collection of characterful houses and cottages.

Kirdford (13)

A peaceful village with a 12th-century church and tiled cottages. In the 16th century it was industrially important with forges and foundries but this is now hard to believe.

Petworth House and Park (15-17)

This magnificent house was built by Charles Seymour, 6th Duke of Somerset, in the late 17th century. Inside the house are some fascinating exhibitions and the North Gallery contains a very important collection of paintings which includes works by Turner (who was a visitor here), Gainsborough and Van Dyke. The 700 acres of deer park were beautifully landscaped by 'Capability' Brown.

Balls Cross

Gunter's Bridge

Petworth

Haslingbourne

Heath End

Selham

South Ambersham

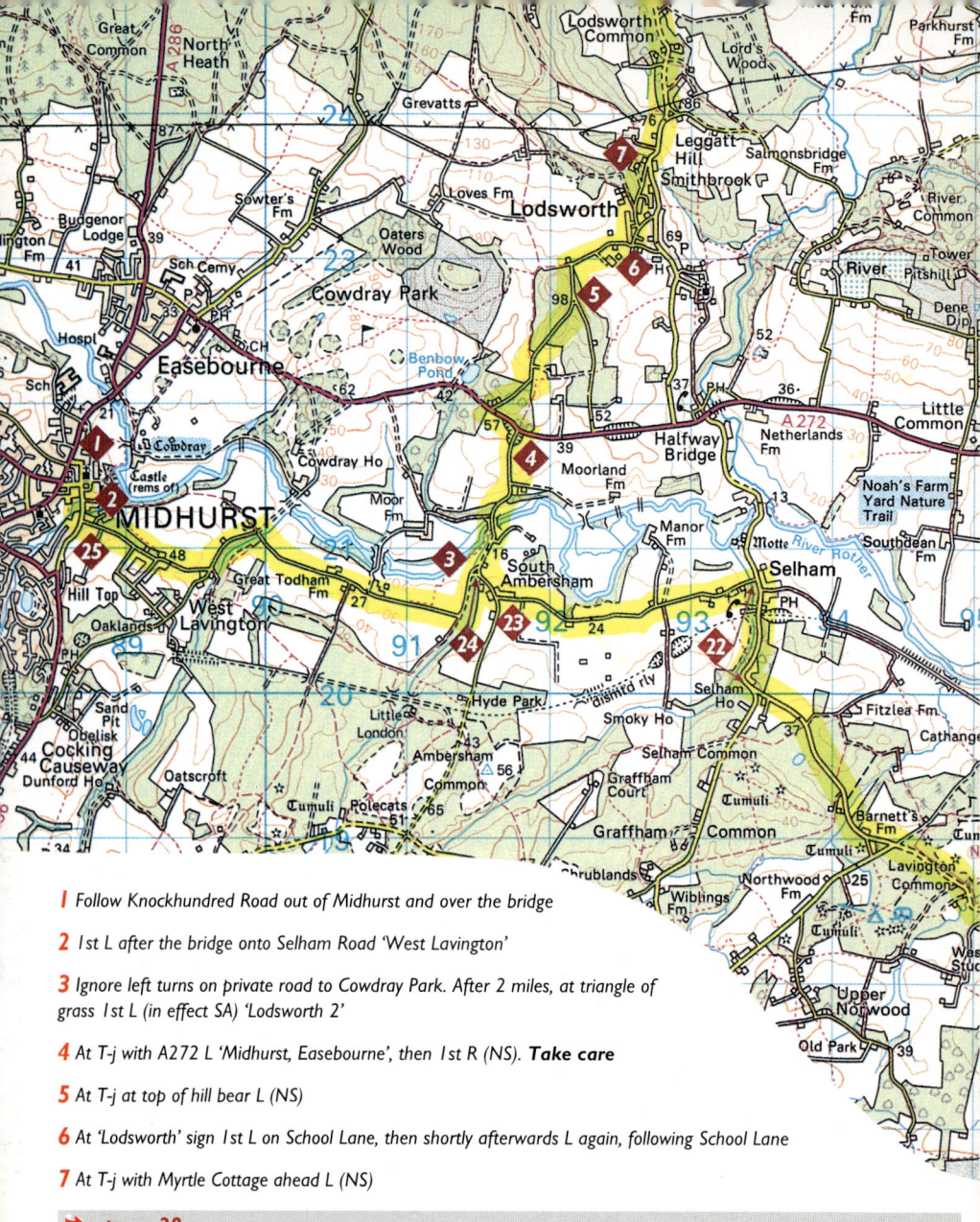

1 Follow Knockhundred Road out of Midhurst and over the bridge

2 1st L after the bridge onto Selham Road 'West Lavington'

3 Ignore left turns on private road to Cowdray Park. After 2 miles, at triangle of grass 1st L (in effect SA) 'Lodsworth 2'

4 At T-j with A272 L 'Midhurst, Easebourne', then 1st R (NS). **Take care**

5 At T-j at top of hill bear L (NS)

6 At 'Lodsworth' sign 1st L on School Lane, then shortly afterwards L again, following School Lane

7 At T-j with Myrtle Cottage ahead L (NS)

➡ **page 28**

15 At T-j with A283 L (NS)

16 In Petworth follow signs for Pulborough A283 until reaching X-roads

17 At X-roads with New Street SA onto Middle Street then at T-j after 100 yards L onto High Street

18 At T-j at end of Grove Lane after almost 1 mile L 'Fittleworth'

19 1st R at X-roads, 'Sutton'

20 At X-roads R 'Duncton'

21 At T-j with A285 L 'Chichester 12, Duncton', then 1st R 'Selham 3 Graffham 3'

22 Just after Three Moles PH in Selham L 'South Ambersham, Midhurst'

23 At T-j R 'Midhurst 3, Lodsworth 3'

24 At triangle of grass L 'West Lavington 1, Midhurst 3'

25 Follow outward route back to start, turning R at T-j to cross bridge back into the centre of Midhurst

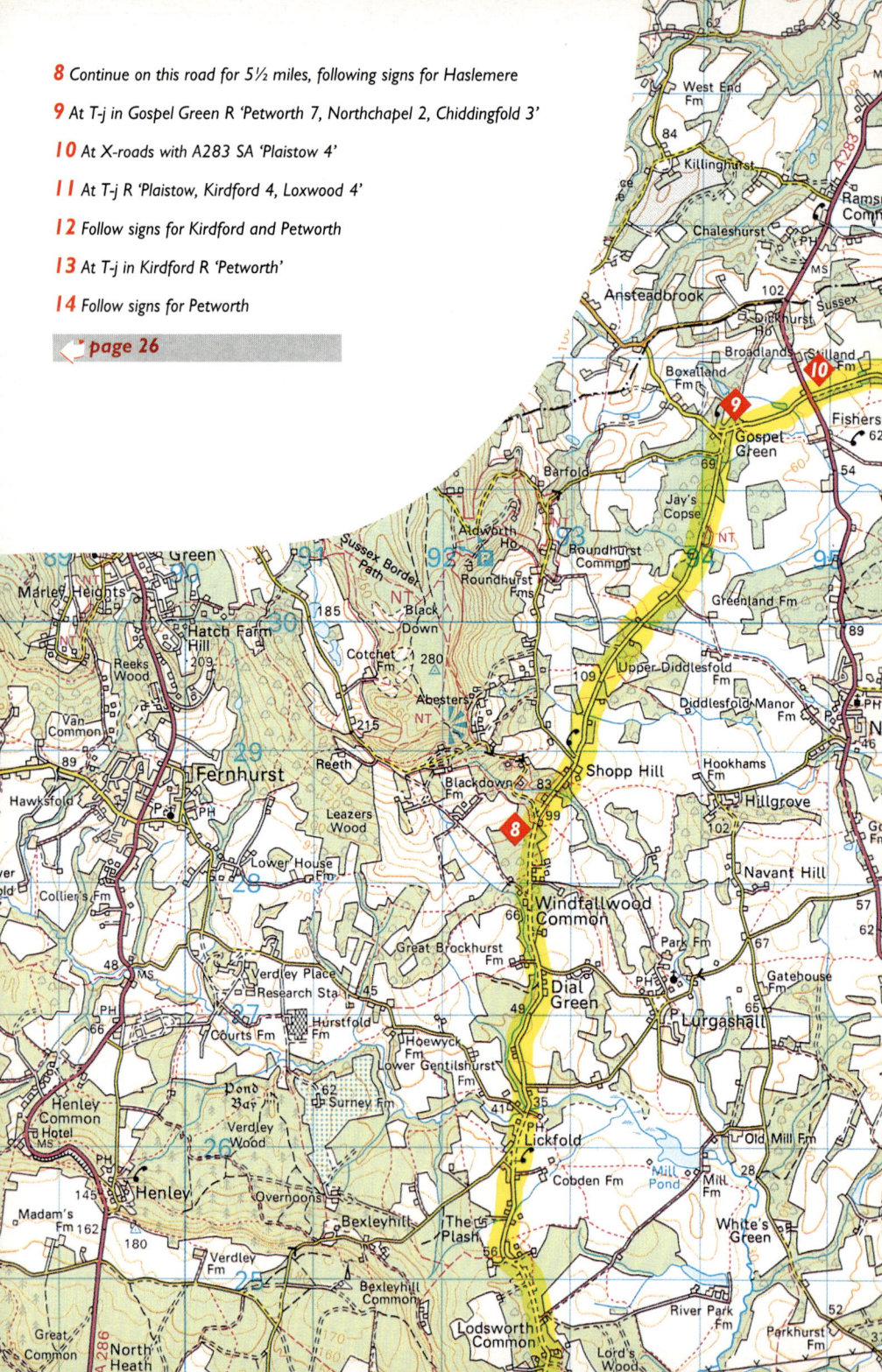

8 Continue on this road for 5½ miles, following signs for Haslemere

9 At T-j in Gospel Green R 'Petworth 7, Northchapel 2, Chiddingfold 3'

10 At X-roads with A283 SA 'Plaistow 4'

11 At T-j R 'Plaistow, Kirdford 4, Loxwood 4'

12 Follow signs for Kirdford and Petworth

13 At T-j in Kirdford R 'Petworth'

14 Follow signs for Petworth

page 26

Chichester and the South Downs

Starting in the striking old Roman town of Chichester, this ride avoids the busy roads to the east of Chichester by linking two no through roads via a short section of footpath, dropping you close to East Lavant. Goodwood House and Country Park are skirted to the east. The ride now meanders over the southwest section of the South Downs, passing through the attractive villages of East Dean, Charlton and Singleton, dropping to cross

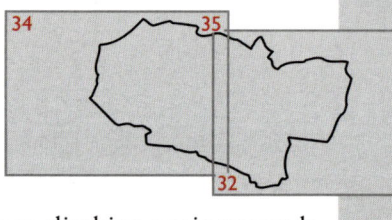

the River Lavant before climbing again towards Chilgrove and the Mardens. The return eastwards back to Chichester is easy, with two enticing detours possible, to Bosham and to Fishbourne Palace.

Start

The Cathedral shop by the Old Tower of Chichester Cathedral

 Follow signs in Chichester

Distance and grade

32 miles

 Easy/moderate

Terrain

The first half of the ride is undulating, the second half flat. A 300-foot climb from Chichester over the downs to East Dean, then several shorter climbs of up to 200 feet, but nothing too serious.

Nearest railway

Chichester, or Rowland's Castle

Refreshments

Plenty of choice in **Chichester**
Hurdlemakers PH ♥, **East Dean**
The Fox PH ♥ ♥, **Charlton**
Fox and Hounds PH, **Singleton**
Selsey Arms PH, **West Dean**
The George PH, **Finchdean**
Several PHs in **Rowland's Castle**

Chichester

Waterbeach

East Dean

Singleton

West Dean

Chilgrove

East Mard.

Chichester (1-3)
This beautiful city with its cathedral and other fine buildings is a centre for both culture and history.

Chichester Cathedral (1)
Built on the site of the shrine of St Richard, this cathedral was consecrated in 1184. It contains both Romanesque stone carvings and modern paintings, sculptures, tapestries and stained glass.

The Pallants (1-2)
These four narrow streets are full of Georgian houses, Pallant House being the most impressive.

Market Cross (1-2)
Chichester's four main streets were laid by the Romans and meet at the Market Cross which was built by Bishop Story in 1501.

Goodwood House (6-7)
Surrounded by parkland, this magnificent late 18th-century house contains beautiful French furniture, porcelain and an important art collection which includes works by Canaletto, Reynolds, Stubbs and Van Dyck. The famous Goodwood racecourse is in the grounds.

Weald and Downland Open Air Museum, Singleton (9-10)
This unusual museum, amidst beautiful Downland scenery, houses restored medieval farmsteads, barns and other agricultural buildings – even a 17th-century watermill in working order.

Stansted Park (21)
This neo-Wren house was the home of the Earl and Countess of Bessborough. It was rebuilt in 1903 but has an ancient chapel, interesting exhibitions and a walled garden. There are wonderful views over the surrounding forest down to the English Channel.

Fishbourne Roman Palace and Museum (26-27)
Fishbourne is the largest Roman residence to have been discovered in Britain. The underfloor heating systems and beautiful mosaic floors can be seen in the remains of the north wing. The gardens have also been restored to their Roman plan.

Littlegreen   Finchdean   Rowland's Castle   Aldsworth   Woodmancote

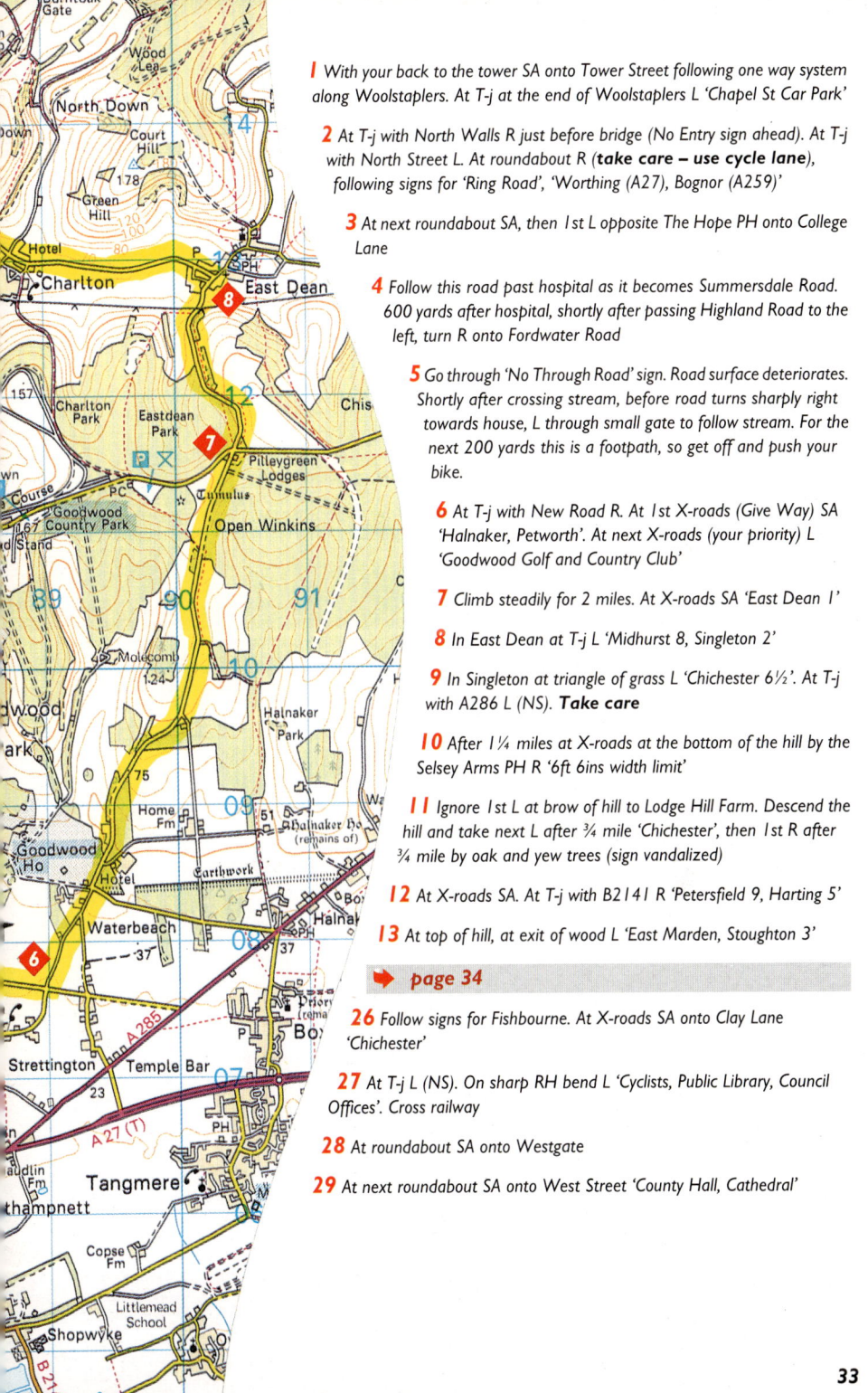

1 With your back to the tower SA onto Tower Street following one way system along Woolstaplers. At T-j at the end of Woolstaplers L 'Chapel St Car Park'

2 At T-j with North Walls R just before bridge (No Entry sign ahead). At T-j with North Street L. At roundabout R (**take care – use cycle lane**), following signs for 'Ring Road', 'Worthing (A27), Bognor (A259)'

3 At next roundabout SA, then 1st L opposite The Hope PH onto College Lane

4 Follow this road past hospital as it becomes Summersdale Road. 600 yards after hospital, shortly after passing Highland Road to the left, turn R onto Fordwater Road

5 Go through 'No Through Road' sign. Road surface deteriorates. Shortly after crossing stream, before road turns sharply right towards house, L through small gate to follow stream. For the next 200 yards this is a footpath, so get off and push your bike.

6 At T-j with New Road R. At 1st X-roads (Give Way) SA 'Halnaker, Petworth'. At next X-roads (your priority) L 'Goodwood Golf and Country Club'

7 Climb steadily for 2 miles. At X-roads SA 'East Dean 1'

8 In East Dean at T-j L 'Midhurst 8, Singleton 2'

9 In Singleton at triangle of grass L 'Chichester 6½'. At T-j with A286 L (NS). **Take care**

10 After 1¼ miles at X-roads at the bottom of the hill by the Selsey Arms PH R '6ft 6ins width limit'

11 Ignore 1st L at brow of hill to Lodge Hill Farm. Descend the hill and take next L after ¾ mile 'Chichester', then 1st R after ¾ mile by oak and yew trees (sign vandalized)

12 At X-roads SA. At T-j with B2141 R 'Petersfield 9, Harting 5'

13 At top of hill, at exit of wood L 'East Marden, Stoughton 3'

➡ **page 34**

26 Follow signs for Fishbourne. At X-roads SA onto Clay Lane 'Chichester'

27 At T-j L (NS). On sharp RH bend L 'Cyclists, Public Library, Council Offices'. Cross railway

28 At roundabout SA onto Westgate

29 At next roundabout SA onto West Street 'County Hall, Cathedral'

13 At top of hill, at exit of wood L 'East Marden, Stoughton 3'

14 In East Marden at thatched well R 'North Marden 1, Harting 4, Compton 3'

15 1st L 'Compton, Up Marden'. Follow up and over hill

16 At fork of roads R 'Harting 3'

17 At T-j with B2146, with oak tree ahead, R uphill (NS), then 1st L opposite Littlegreen School 'Finchdean 3'

18 At T-j L 'Finchdean'

19 At T-j R 'Rowland's Castle 1, Havant 4, Portsmouth 12'

20 After a mile, just before going under railway bridge into Rowland's Castle L opposite the Castle Inn 'Stansted House'

21 At T-j L 'Westbourne 1, Funtington 3, Chichester 8'

22 At top of second short hill, with sign for Common Road on your left, R on Foxbury Lane 'Emsworth, Westbourne' and 1st L on Woodmancote Lane 'Woodmancote'

23 Through Woodmancote and past pub of same name. At T-j L then R onto West Ashling Road, following signs for the Ashlings

24 Just past a row of cream-coloured houses on the right (Edith Cottages) R on Southbrook Road by letter box (NS)

25 At T-j by triangle of grass R 'Bosham, Chichester'

page 33

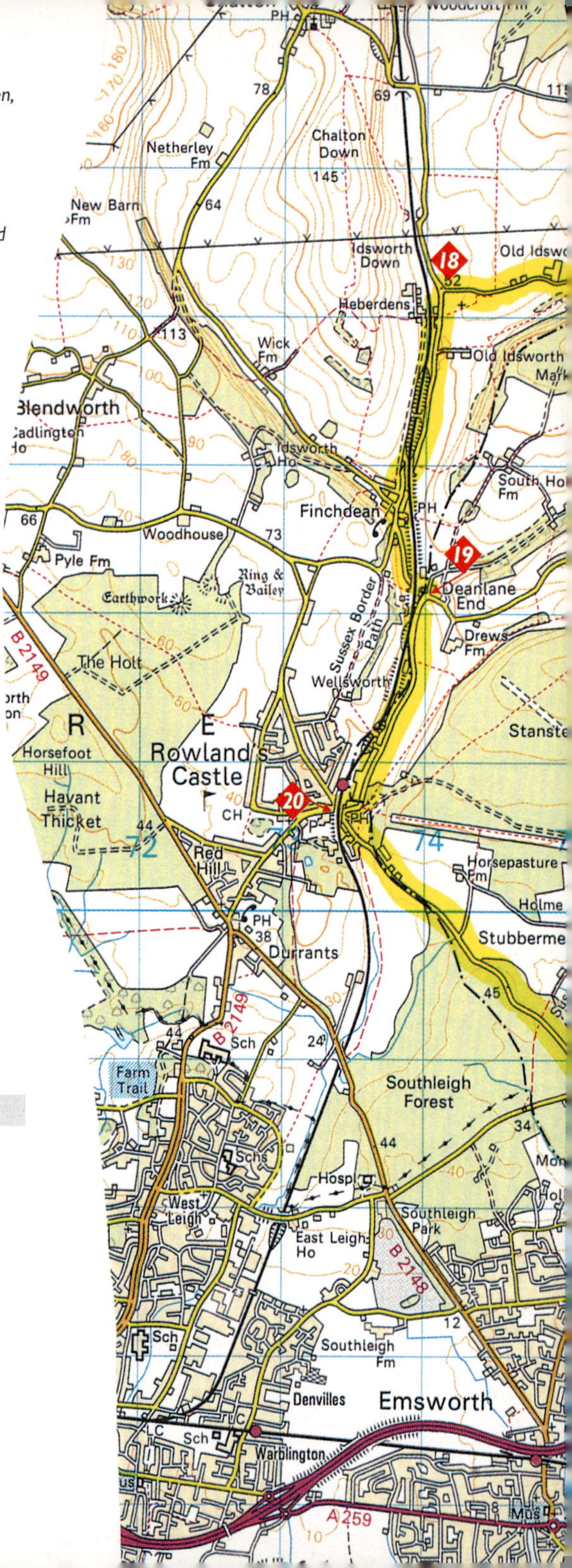

Ruined castles, Roman villas and rough riding west and north of Storrington

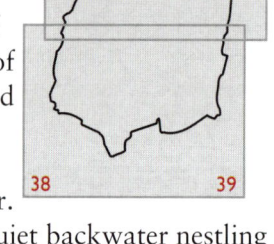

There are two points of interest in the early part of this varied ride: the ruined castle and the whole village of Amberley and the Roman villa at Bignor. Amberley, a delightful quiet backwater nestling beneath the South Downs, has many fine examples of houses built from a wide selection of materials. Bignor Roman Villa has the longest Roman mosaic on display in the country and you can see how the underfloor heating worked. The ride proceeds northwards and neatly avoids spending any time on the A283 by taking a rough but rideable track east of Byworth for a short distance. Passing through various stretches of woodland, the ride describes a loop around Billingshurst before returning to Storrington on quiet lanes.

Start

The White Horse Hotel in the centre of Storrington

P Near the library

Distance and grade

33 miles

Easy/moderate

Terrain

Fairly flat or undulating. One climb of 330 feet from Shopham Bridge over the River Rother south of Byworth to Flexham Park

Nearest railway

Amberley

Refreshments

Lots of choice in **Storrington**
The Sportsman PH ◗, The Black Horse PH ◗, Bridge PH ◗, tea room, **Amberley**
George and Dragon PH ◗◗, **Houghton**
Black Dog and Duck PH ◗, **Bury**
White Horse PH, **Sutton**
Black Horse PH ◗◗ (just off the route), Well Diggers PH, **Byworth**
Foresters PH ◗, Half Moon PH ◗, **Kirdford** (just off the route)
Well Diggers PH, **Byworth**
Cricketers Arms PH, **Wisborough Green**
Bat and Ball Inn, **Newpound Common**
Queens Head PH, **West Chiltington**

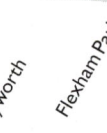

Storrington   Rackham   Cross Gate   Amberley   Bury   West Burton   Bignor   Sutton   Byworth   Flexham Park

Parham House, Pulborough (3-4)
Built in the late 16th century but with 18th-century additions, this grey stone, gabled house lies in an ancient deer park. The gardens were designed more recently and include walled gardens, a fountain and red water-lily pond and a temple garden. Inside the house are original carved panellings and Tudor and Jacobean furniture.

Amberley (6)
An attractive village with twisting streets full of a variety of cottages, thatched, timbered, brick, stone and flint. The ruins of Amberley Castle, a former retreat of the Bishop of Chichester, and a Norman church stand on the edge of the village. The old Black Horse Inn is practically a museum with its collections of sheep bells and shepherds' crooks.

Mosaic floor at Bignor

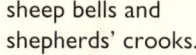

Amberley Chalk Pits Museum (6-7)
This huge industrial museum is set in a 36-acre former chalk quarry with much of the original machinery on display. Other crafts and industries are demonstrated in workshops and visitors can travel around the area on the narrow gauge railway or the workmen's train.

Bignor (11)
Some of the finest mosaic floors discovered outside Italy can be seen in the remains of this large Roman villa. The museum is also interesting and the surrounding countryside is beautiful.

Wisborough Green
Newpound Common
Coneyhurst
Broadford Bridge
West Chiltington

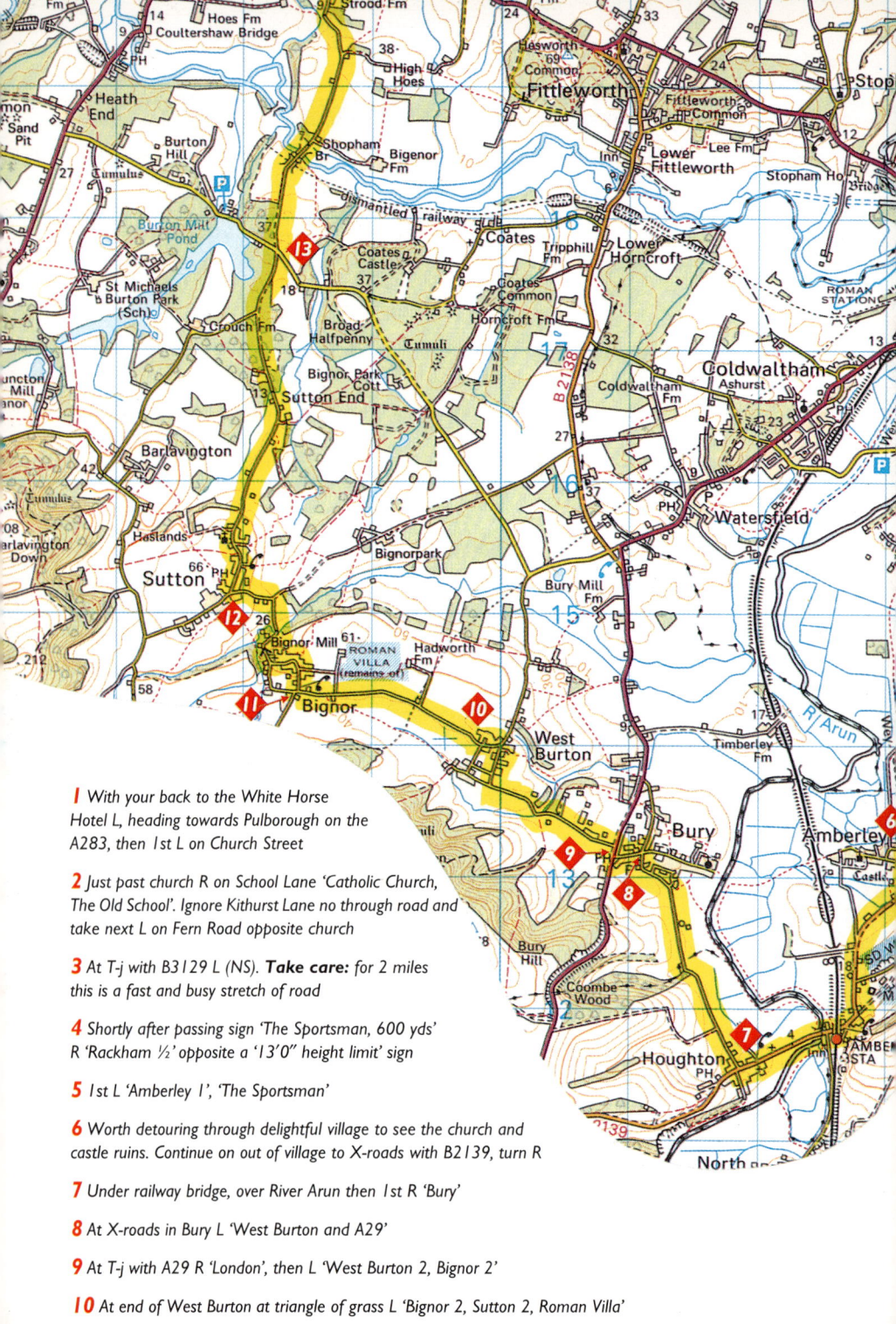

1 With your back to the White Horse Hotel L, heading towards Pulborough on the A283, then 1st L on Church Street

2 Just past church R on School Lane 'Catholic Church, The Old School'. Ignore Kithurst Lane no through road and take next L on Fern Road opposite church

3 At T-j with B3129 L (NS). **Take care:** for 2 miles this is a fast and busy stretch of road

4 Shortly after passing sign 'The Sportsman, 600 yds' R 'Rackham ½' opposite a '13′0″ height limit' sign

5 1st L 'Amberley 1', 'The Sportsman'

6 Worth detouring through delightful village to see the church and castle ruins. Continue on out of village to X-roads with B2139, turn R

7 Under railway bridge, over River Arun then 1st R 'Bury'

8 At X-roads in Bury L 'West Burton and A29'

9 At T-j with A29 R 'London', then L 'West Burton 2, Bignor 2'

10 At end of West Burton at triangle of grass L 'Bignor 2, Sutton 2, Roman Villa'

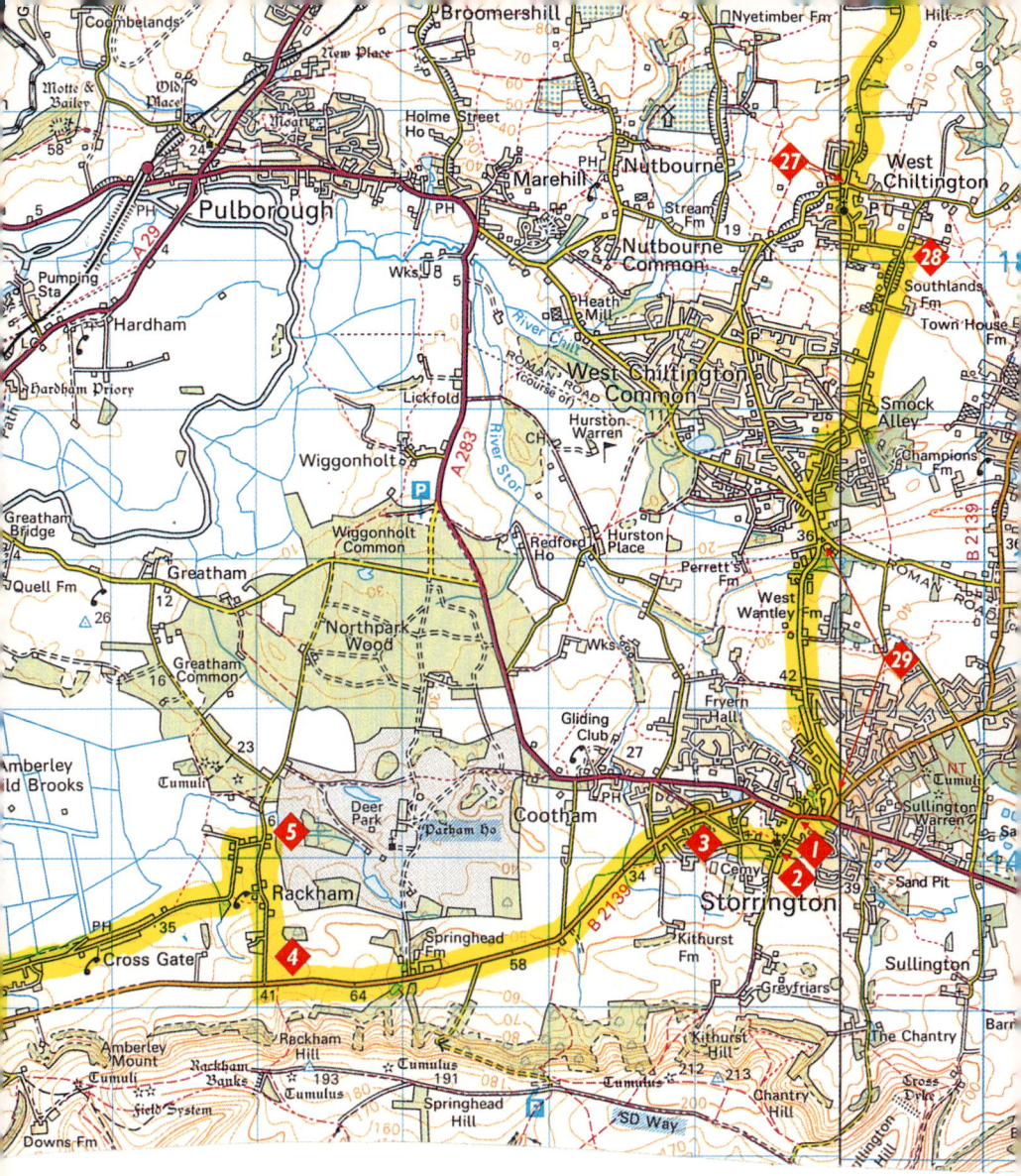

11 In Bignor follow signs for 'Sutton, Duncton'

12 At the White Horse PH in Sutton follow road uphill 'Byworth, Petworth'

13 At X-roads SA 'Petworth 3'

➜ **page 40**

27 At X-roads in West Chiltington by Queens Head PH SA onto Church Street

28 At T-j R on Southlands Lane

29 This road becomes Smock Alley then Roundabout Lane and passes Five Bells PH. At T-j L (sign vandalized), then at T-j with B2139 R to return to Storrington

14 At offset X-roads SA 'Byworth'

15 **Easy to miss**. Just past brow of hill in Byworth, opposite stone and red-brick barn with large grey wooden doors R onto **track** through farm. The track is rideable.

16 Emerge at X-roads on A283 by Well Diggers PH. SA (NS)

17 Follow signs for 'Kirdford, Plaistow'. At X-roads with A272 SA 'Plaistow 6'

18 In Kirdford just past Half Moon PH follow road round 'Wisborough Green 2'

19 At X-roads in Wisborough Green SA 'Newpound'

20 At T-j with B2133 R (NS)

21 At T-j with A272 L 'Billingshurst', then 1st L after bridge 'Gallery 2'

22 Ignore 1st right to Tedfold Stud Farm. Go under power lines and into wood. ½ mile after start of wood 1st R 'Gallery ½'

23 At T-j with A29 R 'Billingshurst 1, (use pavement/cyclepath), then 2nd L 'Barns Green 3'

24 At T-j R 'Coneyhurst 2'

25 At T-j with A272 L 'Cowfold', then 1st R by telephone box onto West Chiltington Lane

26 At T-j with B2133 L 'Thakeham, Ashington', then 1st R on Broadford Bridge Road 'West Chiltington'

← **page 39**

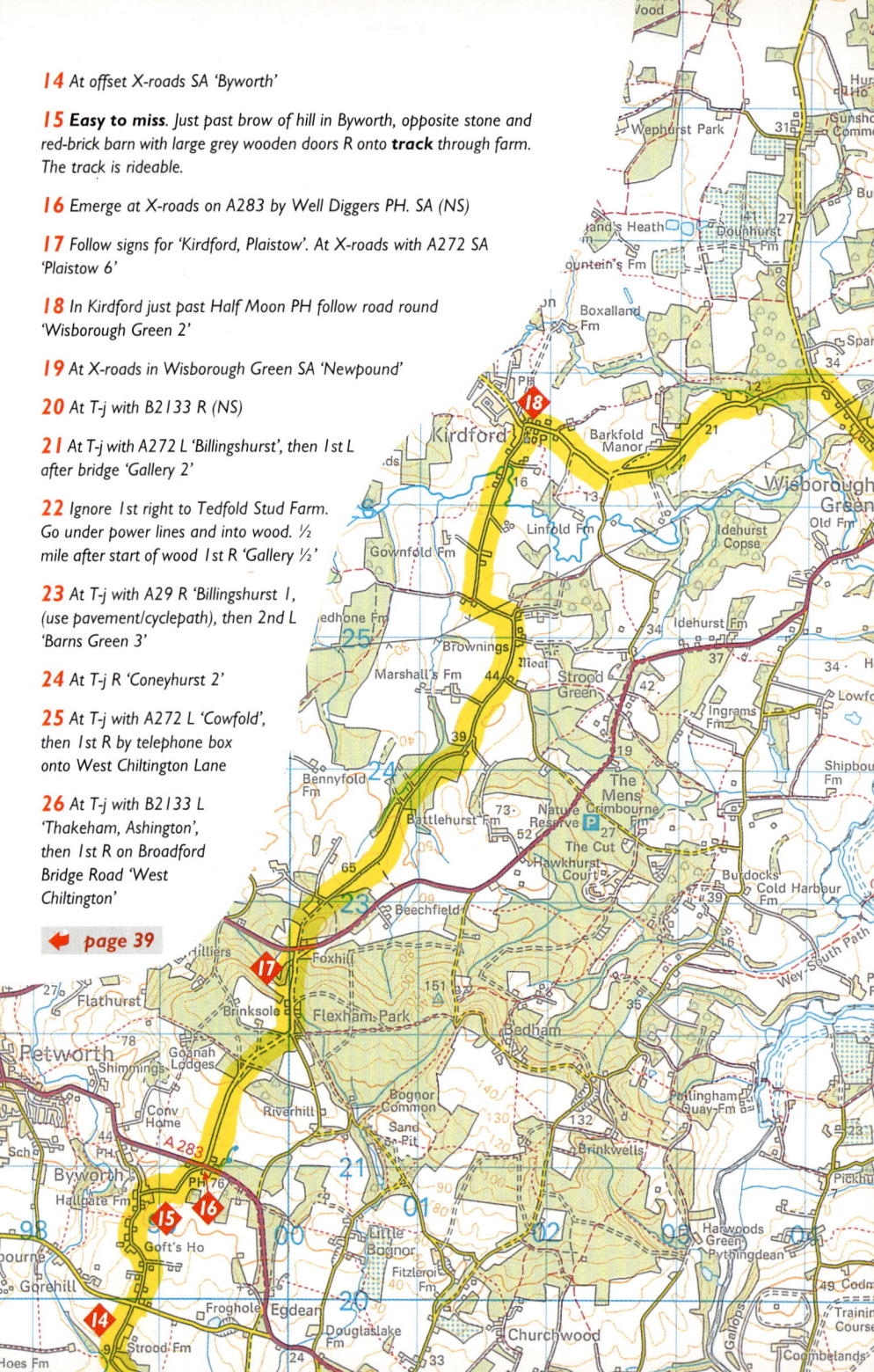

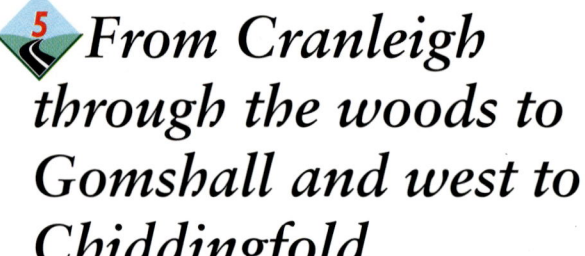

5 *From Cranleigh through the woods to Gomshall and west to Chiddingfold*

Start

Stocklund Square, by the clock and fountain, Cranleigh

 Follow signs

Distance and grade

37 miles

Moderate/strenuous

Terrain

A steep climb (almost 600 feet) from Cranleigh to Winterfold Wood and a shorter, 230-foot hill from Brook to Farley Heath. Lots of short, sharp climbs between Shamley Green and Dunsfold

Nearest railway

Gomshall or Witley, 1½ miles west of Hambledon

Lovely woodland, quiet lanes and old villages make this one of the best areas close to southwest London for cycling in real countryside. The first climb, through the woods north of Cranleigh, is fairly unforgiving, but the woodland is very beautiful and it is at the start of the ride! Fine refreshment stop at Gomshall Mill and several pubs along the way at Hascombe, Hambledon, Chiddingfold and Dunsfold. The route manages to avoid busy roads almost entirely, making use at one point of a paved bridleway west of the A281. The ride can easily be linked with the next one, east of Cranleigh, to form a 60-mile route.

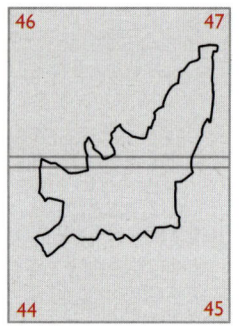

Refreshments

Lots of choice in **Cranleigh**
Compass Inn PH, Gomshall Mill for coffee and tea, **Gomshall**
White Horse Inn, Prince of Wales PH, **Shere**
William IV PH, **Albury Heath**
White Horse PH, **Hascombe** (just off the route)
Merry Harriers PH, **Hambledon**
Swan PH, Crown PH (also does teas), **Chiddingfold**
Sun PH, **Dunsfold**

Cranleigh   Winterfold Wood   Burrows Cross   Gomshall   Shere   Brook   Farley   Shamley Green   Thorncombe Street

Shere (8)

Said to be Surrey's prettiest village, Shere consists of timbered houses and cottages built along the willow-covered banks of a stream. The church is notable for its octagonal spire and Norman tower. Among the many well-preserved old buildings, the Oak Cottage and the White Horse Inn are of particular interest.

Chiddingfold

Winkworth Arboretum (18-19)

95 acres of hillside woodland gardens with rare shrubs and trees and two lakes.

Hascombe (19-20)

Lying in a valley between wooded hills, this village is full of attractive, old cottages. One of the surrounding ridges, Telegraph Hill, was used as a signalling station during the Napoleonic Wars.

Oakhurst Cottage, Hambledon (22)

This 16th-century, timber-framed cottage has been restored and furnished authentically.

Chiddingfold (23)

An important centre for glass until the 16th century, this village has records of the earliest glass blower, Lawrence, in 1227. The Church of St Mary, overlooking the central green, has only one window of Chiddingfold glass but is interesting nevertheless. Opposite the church is the Crown Inn, one of the oldest inns in the country; it was built as a rest home for Cistercian Monks and became an inn in 1383.

Hascombe

Hambledon

Chiddingfold

Highstreet Green

Dunsfold

1 With your back to the fountain R along High Street. At roundabout by obelisk L on Ewhurst Road 'Ewhurst 2, Ockley 6'

2 After ¾ mile, opposite telephone box L on Barhatch Lane 'Albury 6, Shere 5'

➡ **page 46**

19 At T-j with B2130 L 'Hascombe, Dunsfold', then 1st R on Mare Lane '6ft 6ins width limit' (or SA for the White Horse PH)

20 Steep climb then descent. At T-j at bottom of hill by triangle of grass R (NS)

21 At X-roads L 'Hambledon, Chiddingfold'

22 Ignore 1st left to Hambledon Church, take next L opposite house called Bryony Hill 'Pockford, Dunsfold', then at T-j L (NS)

23 After 3 miles, at T-j in Chiddingfold R for pubs (Crown also does teas), shop and village green, or L on Pickhurst Road to continue route

24 *After I mile Ist L on High Street Green 'Dunsfold, Cranleigh'*

25 *At beginning of Dunsfold, opposite The Sun PH by memorial cross R onto Alfold Road 'Alfold, Horsham'*

26 *Follow signs for Alfold and Horsham. At T-j with A281 L 'Guildford', then Ist R* **take care** *onto Wildwood Lane 'Cranleigh 2, Ewhurst 4'*

27 *At T-j at the end of Wildwood Lane L 'Cranleigh'. (If you wish to turn this into a 60-mile ride by linking with route 6, east of Cranleigh, turn R at this T-j 'Baynards ½, joining next route in middle of instruction 2)*

28 *At T-j in Cranleigh R to return to starting point*

3 Steep then even steeper climb through lovely woodland. At T-j R 'Ewhurst, Cranleigh', then after 400 yards 1st L 'Peaslake'

4 During the long descent, after 1½ miles 1st L on Lawbrook Lane by large yellow grit bin

5 At T-j at the end of Lawbrook Lane L, then R on Burrows Lane 'Gomshall, Dorking'

6 Follow signs for Dorking down into Gomshall. At T-j with A25 L 'Shere, Guildford'

7 2nd L 'Shere ¼, Ewhurst 5½, Cranleigh 7½'

8 In Shere 1st L onto Middle Street 'Ewhurst, Cranleigh'

9 Climb steadily for ¾ mile. Just before crossing red-brick bridge over railway, at small triangle of grass R 'Farley Green, Albury'

10 By large triangle of grass 1st L onto Little London 'Farley Green, Shamley Green'

11 At T-j with Brook Hill L 'Farley Green, Shamley Green'

12 After 2 miles, having gone up and over hill, shortly after passing Madgehole Lane (no through road) on your left next L by pond onto Stroud Lane 'Cranleigh. Unsuitable for HGV'

13 At end of Stroud Lane, at T-j with B2128 R 'Shamley Green, Guildford', then L on Upper House Lane

14 At T-j by triangle of grass with large red-brick house ahead R (NS)

15 At T-j with A281 R 'Bramley 1, Guildford 5' (use pavement if the road is very busy). **Easy to miss** 1st L just before sign for Birtley Green, onto public bridleway 'Private Road, Brookwell'

16 Bear R past black iron gates. At T-J by small red-brick corner cottage with pond ahead turn L

17 At end of Gate Street R 'Thorncombe St 1¾, Godalming 4¾'

18 **Easy to miss** After 1½ miles, just after beautiful half-timbered, honey-coloured house L 'Arboretum, Hascombe'

19 At T-j with B2130 L 'Hascombe, Dunsfold', then 1st R on Mare Lane '6ft 6ins width limit' (or SA for the White Horse PH)

◀ **page 44**

6 *Quiet lanes, woodland and Leith Hill, east from Cranleigh*

A ride of two contrasting sections: the first half is flatter, more open and devoted to farmland; the second half climbs steeply into woodland with the opportunity of going to the very top of Leith Hill for magnificent views over the surrounding countryside. Some of the quieter lanes such as those between Oakwoodhill and Ockley Station, are the truly perfect cycling environment. By contrast there is one difficult junction off the A29 towards Leith Hill. Please read instruction 11 carefully.

52		53
50		51

Start

Stocklund Square, at the clock and fountain, Cranleigh

P Follow signs

Distance and grade

28 miles

 Moderate

Terrain

Flat or undulating as far as Capel, then a major climb of 550 feet to Leith Hill. The road from Peaslake to Ewhurst takes the easiest line, avoiding a big climb

Nearest railway

Ockley, or Gomshall, 2 miles from northwest tip of route

Cranleigh

Cox Green

Oakwoodhill

Ockley Station

Capel

Places of interest

Leith Hill Tower (12-13)
Built in the 18th century, this tower marks the highest point in southeast England and there are wonderful views over the downs. The rhododendron wood is also worth visiting.

Refreshments

Lots of choice in **Cranleigh**
Thurlow Arms PH, **Baynards**
Punchbowl PH ✿ ✿, **Oakwoodhill**
Crown Inn, **Capel**
The Plough PH ✿ ✿, **Coldharbour**
Abinger Hatch ✿, **Abinger Common**
Volunteer Inn ✿, **Sutton Abinger**
Hurtwood Inn, **Peaslake**
Bulls Head PH ✿, **Ewhurst**

Friday Street (14)
Slightly off the route and approached through beautiful woodland is the hamlet of Friday Street. Comprising a lake, a few cottages and an inn, it is subject to a preservation order that helps it to retain its remoteness and tranquility. The Evelyn family (descendants of John Evelyn) are Lords of the Manor and own many of the cottages as homes for those working on the estate.

Abinger Common (16)
Possibly the oldest village in England, a Mesolithic Pit Dwelling dating from 5000-4000 BC was unearthed here and is the oldest preserved, man-made dwelling in the country. Nearby is the church, which was bombed during the Second World War leaving only the 13th-century chapel intact; the stocks still stand on the green in the front. There are many literary connections: the manor house was built by the 17th-century diarist John Evelyn, Sir Max Beerbohm lived at Manor Cottage and E M Forster wrote a collection of essays entitled 'Abinger Harvest'.

Coldharbour

Leith Hill

Abinger Common

Sutton Abinger

Peaslake

Ewhurst

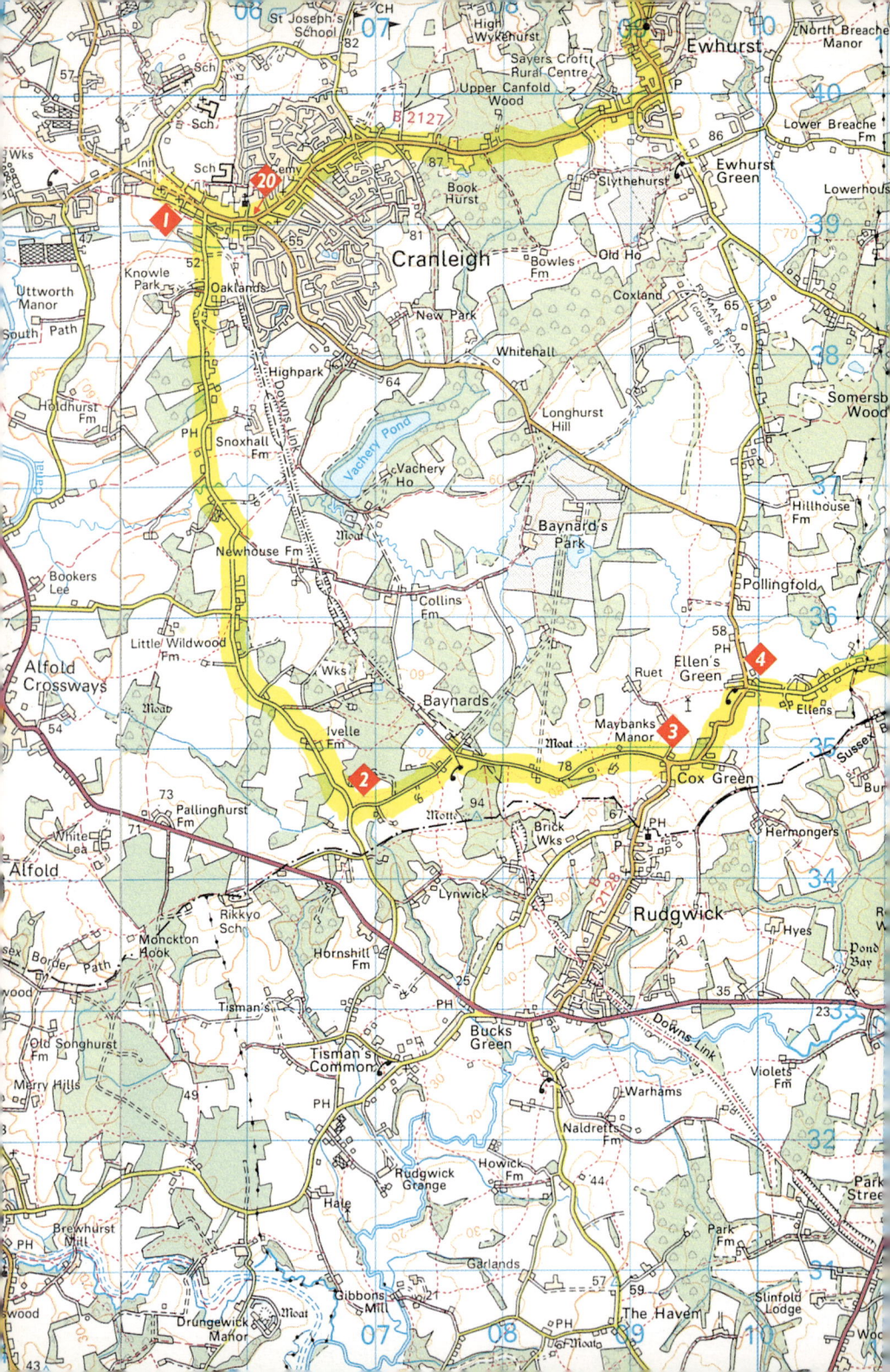

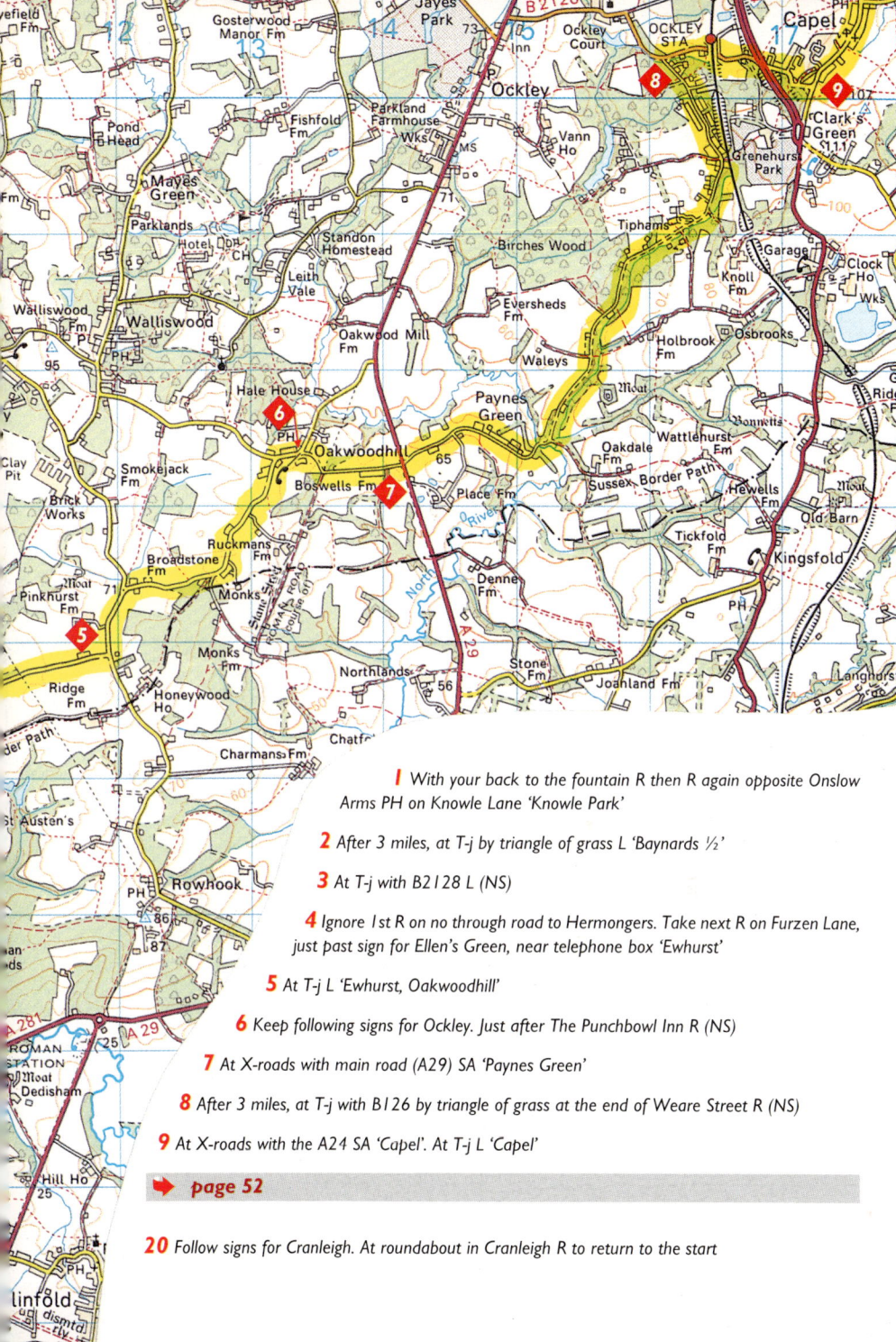

1 With your back to the fountain R then R again opposite Onslow Arms PH on Knowle Lane 'Knowle Park'

2 After 3 miles, at T-j by triangle of grass L 'Baynards ½'

3 At T-j with B2128 L (NS)

4 Ignore 1st R on no through road to Hermongers. Take next R on Furzen Lane, just past sign for Ellen's Green, near telephone box 'Ewhurst'

5 At T-j L 'Ewhurst, Oakwoodhill'

6 Keep following signs for Ockley. Just after The Punchbowl Inn R (NS)

7 At X-roads with main road (A29) SA 'Paynes Green'

8 After 3 miles, at T-j with B126 by triangle of grass at the end of Weare Street R (NS)

9 At X-roads with the A24 SA 'Capel'. At T-j L 'Capel'

➡ **page 52**

20 Follow signs for Cranleigh. At roundabout in Cranleigh R to return to the start

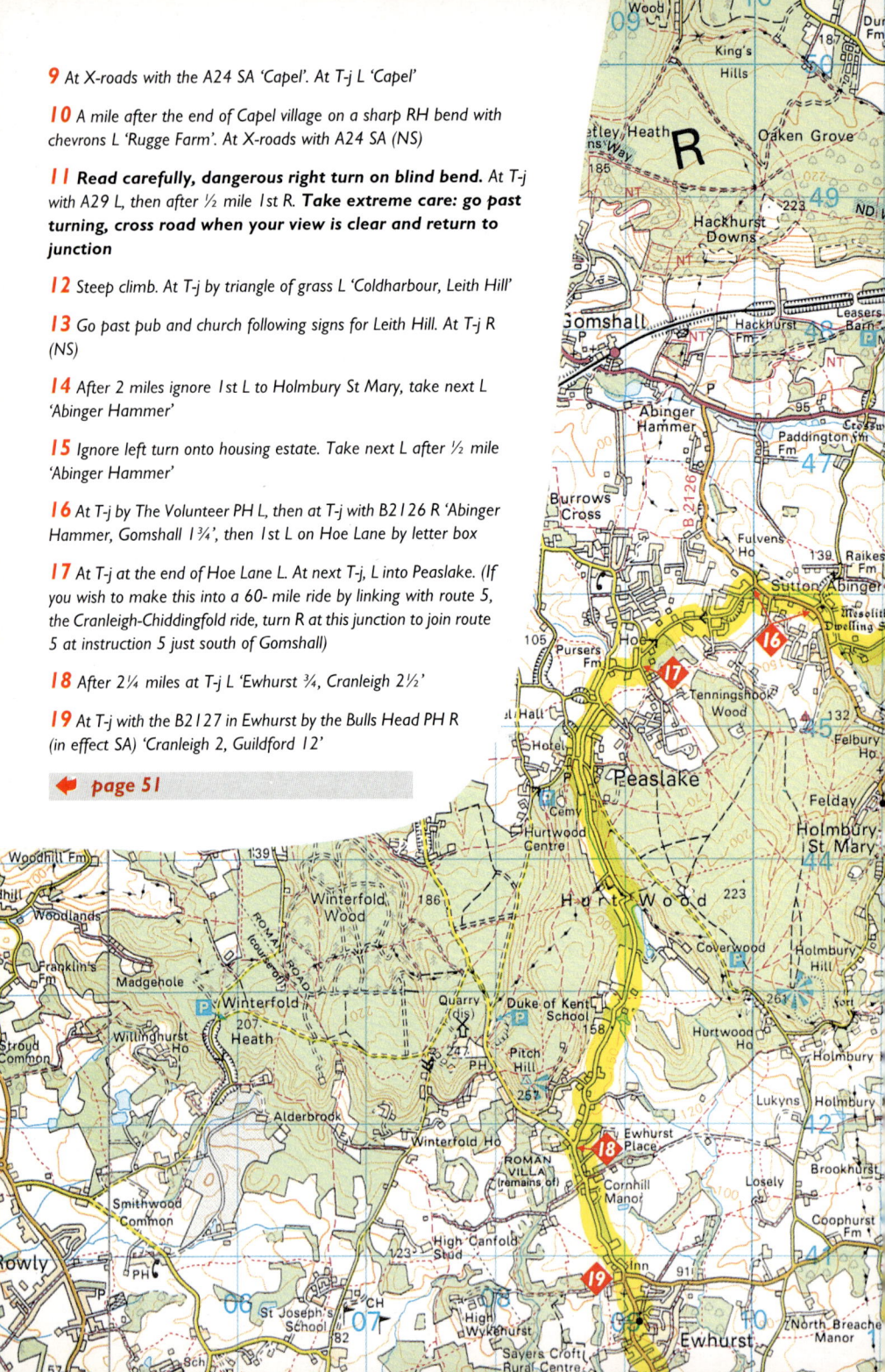

9 At X-roads with the A24 SA 'Capel'. At T-j L 'Capel'

10 A mile after the end of Capel village on a sharp RH bend with chevrons L 'Rugge Farm'. At X-roads with A24 SA (NS)

11 **Read carefully, dangerous right turn on blind bend.** At T-j with A29 L, then after ½ mile 1st R. **Take extreme care: go past turning, cross road when your view is clear and return to junction**

12 Steep climb. At T-j by triangle of grass L 'Coldharbour, Leith Hill'

13 Go past pub and church following signs for Leith Hill. At T-j R (NS)

14 After 2 miles ignore 1st L to Holmbury St Mary, take next L 'Abinger Hammer'

15 Ignore left turn onto housing estate. Take next L after ½ mile 'Abinger Hammer'

16 At T-j by The Volunteer PH L, then at T-j with B2126 R 'Abinger Hammer, Gomshall 1¾', then 1st L on Hoe Lane by letter box

17 At T-j at the end of Hoe Lane L. At next T-j, L into Peaslake. (If you wish to make this into a 60- mile ride by linking with route 5, the Cranleigh-Chiddingfold ride, turn R at this junction to join route 5 at instruction 5 just south of Gomshall)

18 After 2¼ miles at T-j L 'Ewhurst ¾, Cranleigh 2½'

19 At T-j with the B2127 in Ewhurst by the Bulls Head PH R (in effect SA) 'Cranleigh 2, Guildford 12'

← **page 51**

From Edenbridge via the North Downs to Lingfield

The route leaves the valley formed by Eden Brook to climb through woodland skirting Oxted. Crossing first the A25 then the M25, you climb onto the North Downs and follow the ridge westwards. Dropping down to Godstone, the route continues southwards to Lingfield. Race against the horses and leave them in your wake as you enter the lovely network of lanes southeast from Dormansland. The route passes close to Hever Castle, childhood home of Anne Boleyn.

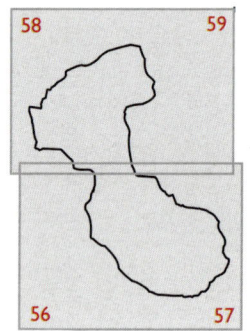

Start

White Horse PH, High Street, Edenbridge

P Follow signs

Distance and grade

33 miles

 Moderate

Terrain

Three major climbs: 400 feet from Edenbridge to Limpsfield Chart, 450 feet from the A25 to Botley Hill and 330 feet from Lingfield to southeast of Dormansland

Nearest railway

Edenbridge

Refreshments

Plenty of choice, **Edenbridge**
Plenty of choice, **Godstone**
Fox and Hounds, **south of Godstone**
Brickmakers Arms, **Crowhurst Lane End**
Hare and Hounds ●, **north of Lingfield**
Star PH, Old Cage PH ●, **Lingfield**
Fountain PH ●, Crown PH, **Cowden**
Kentish Horse PH, Greyhound PH, **Markbeech**

Link with route 8

*Either leave this route at instruction 9 and follow link on page 61 to join route 8 at instruction 22 **or** leave at instruction 24 and join route 8 at instruction 4*

Edenbridge   Troy Town   Pains Hill   Limpsfield Chart   Moorhouse Bank   Botley Hill   South Hawke   Godstone

Haxted Watermill and Museum (2)

Slightly off the route, this watermill was built in 1580 and has been restored to working order.

Detillens, Limpsfield (5)

A Georgian front conceals a 15th-century timbered house. There is a Tudor morning room and a Jacobean staircase and the original central truss can still be seen in the main bedroom. An interesting collection of guns, decorations and orders is on display.

Hever Castle

Squerryes Court (7)

Built in 1681, this William and Mary manor house contains an interesting collection of English paintings, porcelain, tapestries and furniture from the 18th century and some important Dutch old masters. The gardens have been landscaped and include a lake, formal gardens, woodland walks and an original 18th-century dovecote.

Bletchingley (14)

Slightly off the route, this pretty village is full of attractive period cottages, notably Nicholas Wolmer's which dates back to 1552. The Whyte Hart Inn, probably the oldest building, was built in 1388. The church contains some interesting monuments.

Hever Castle (26-27)

Most famous as the childhood home of Anne Boleyn, this castle dates back to 1270 when the Gatehouse, outer walls and moat were built. In the 15th century, the Boleyn family added a Tudor home within the walls. The Astors acquired the estate in the early 20th century and restored the castle and the gardens as well as building a mock Tudor village. The house is full of the fine pictures and furniture that they collected.

Crowhurst   Lingfield   Dormansland   Cowden   Markbeech

1 With your back to the White Horse PH L then 1st major L on Stangrove Road 'Haxted, Golf Course'

2 At T-j with Crouch House Road R 'Golf Course'

3 Ignore 1st right after 1 mile on Hilders Lane. After further ½ mile, having passed through Little Brown and crossed a bridge over a small stream, R by a triangle of grass 'Pains Hill, Limpsfield, Chart'

➡ **page 59**

18 After 2½ miles, at offset X-roads SA on Crowhurst Road 'Lingfield, Dormansland', then 1st R on Saxby's Road 'Lingfield'

19 Past the Star PH and the church. At X-roads L on Town Hill

20 1st R after going under railway bridge on Dormans Road 'Dormansland, East Grinstead'

21 At X-roads SA onto Hollow Lane 'Cowden, Tunbridge Wells'

22 Climb two hills. On the second descent, shortly after a telephone box and sharp RH bend with chevrons next L by triangle of grass '6ft 6ins width limit'

23 Lovely stretch. After 2 miles at T-j L 'Cowden'

24 At X-roads with B2026 SA 'Cowden Station ½, Penshurst 5'. (If you are going to do route 8 as well take the 1st R 'Moat Lane' to join it at instruction 4)

25 After going under railway bridge, at top of steep hill, with large red-brick house ahead, L (sign broken)

26 At X-roads by Kentish Horse PH SA 'Hever, Chiddingstone'

27 At T-j with the High Street in Edenbridge by the Star Inn R to return to start

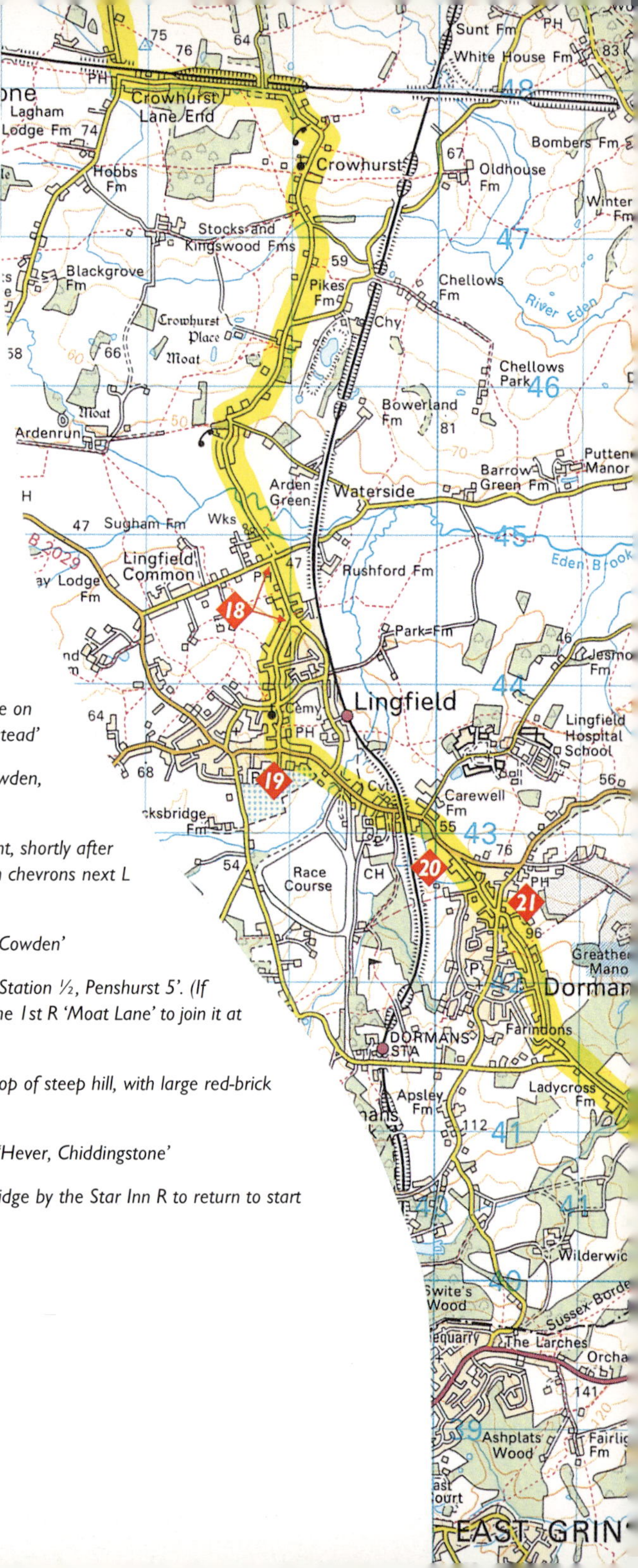

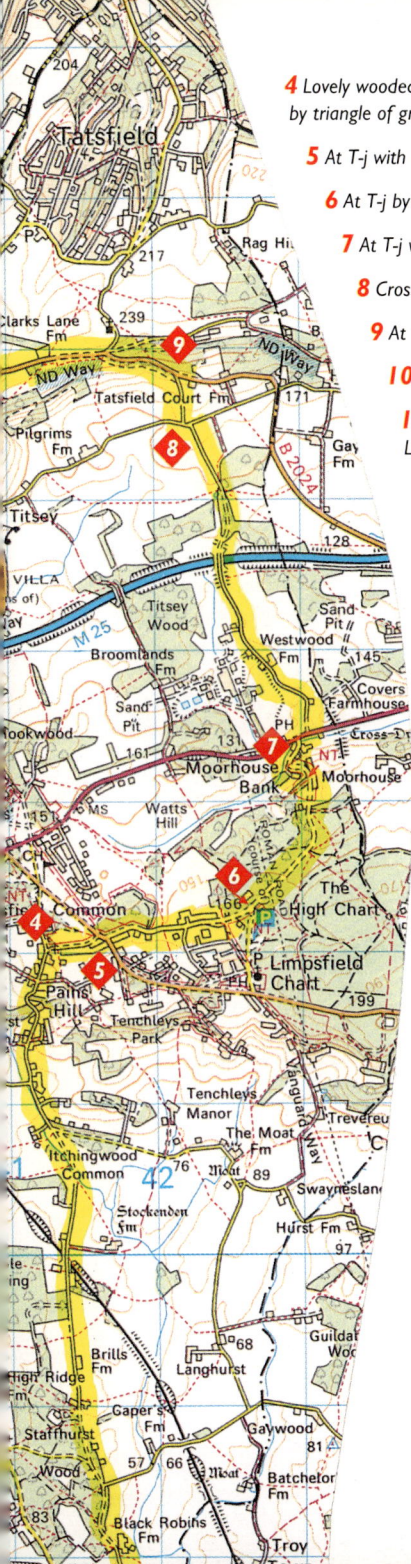

4 *Lovely wooded section. Follow signs for Pains Hill. After 2 miles, steep climb. At brow by triangle of grass and a letter box set in a brick pillar R (NS)*

5 *At T-j with B269 R, then L on Ridlands Lane*

6 *At T-j by National Trust sign for Limpsfield Common L downhill*

7 *At T-j with A25 by Grasshopper PH R, then L on Clacket Lane*

8 *Cross M25. At T-j L then R (NS)*

9 *At T-j with B2024 L (NS)*

10 *At T-j with B269 R, then L on The Ridge 'Woldingham 2½'*

11 *After 1½ miles, on sharp RH bend with chevrons by the golf course L on Gangers Hill*

12 *At T-j with A25 R, then at roundabout L 'Godstone'*

13 *At the bottom of the main street bear L (in effect SA) 'Godstone Farm'*

14 *Shortly after the Bell PH R on Tilburstow Hill 'Tilburstow Hill I'*

15 *Climb and descend hill. Just after Fox and Hounds PH L 'South Godstone, Tandridge'*

16 *At X-roads with A22 SA onto Miles Lane 'Tandridge, Crowhurst'*

17 *Following signs for Crowhurst, at T-j with Tandridge Lane R 'Crowhurst, Lingfield' then 1st L immediately after railway bridge by the Brickmakers Arms onto Crowhurst Lane End 'Crowhurst'*

← **page 56**

8 *East of Edenbridge*

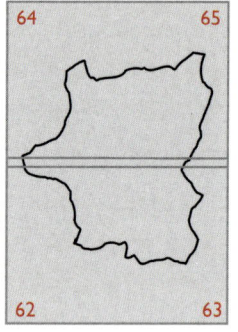

64   65

62   63

Escape into the country-side on this ride that passes close to both Tunbridge Wells and Sevenoaks but takes you along tiny lanes made for cycling. After passing through the delights of Speldhurst and Leigh you are soon faced with the demanding 600-foot hill, with one particularly steep section beyond Underriver. Still, it is beautiful woodland and does it really matter if you get off and push? Having gained this height, you stay on the ridge until The Chart, after which there is a fast descent to Four Elms, then a 3-mile stretch of a fairly busy road to return to the start. For a longer ride follow the link on the facing page and return to Edenbridge from the west.

Start

White Horse PH, High Street, Edenbridge

 P Follow signs

Distance and grade

30 miles

 Moderate

Terrain

Two major climbs: 370 feet from Edenbridge to Marlbeech, 600 feet from Leigh to Hubbards Hill, with a steep section of 270 feet in less than 1 mile to the north of Underriver

Nearest railway

Edenbridge

Refreshments

Plenty of choice, **Edenbridge**
Kentish Horse PH, **Markbeech**
Chafford Arms PH, **Fordcombe**
George and Dragon PH, **Speldhurst**
Fleur de Lis PH, Bat and Ball PH, **Leigh**
Gate PH, **Leigh Station**
White Rock, **Underriver**
Cock Inn PH, Crown PH, **Ide Hill**

Edenbridge

Markbeech
Horseshoe Green

White Post

Fordcombe

Speldhurst

Leigh

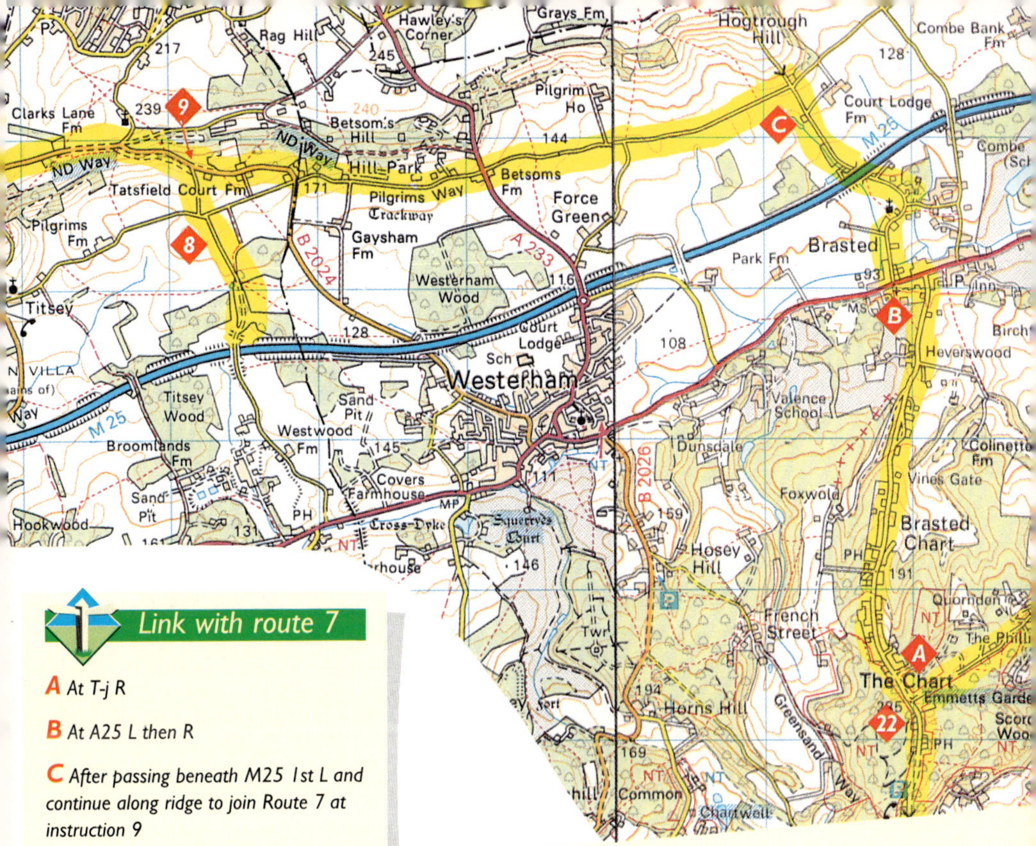

Link with route 7

A At T-j R

B At A25 L then R

C After passing beneath M25 1st L and continue along ridge to join Route 7 at instruction 9

Places of interest

Chiddingstone village and castle (1-2)
The village is owned by the National Trust and has a street full of well-preserved 16th- and 17th-century houses. The castle was built in 1679 and was castellated 'Gothic-style' in the early 19th century.

Penshurst Place (11)
This grand medieval manor house dates back to 1341 and was the home of the Elizabethan poet Sir Philip Sidney. There are formal gardens, an adventure playground and a toy museum.

Knole (16-17)
Set around 7 courtyards and surrounded by parkland, this huge house is almost like a village. It was built in the 15th century by Thomas Bouchier, Archbishop of Canterbury

Underriver Hubbard's Hill Ide Hill The Chart Toy's Hill Four Elms

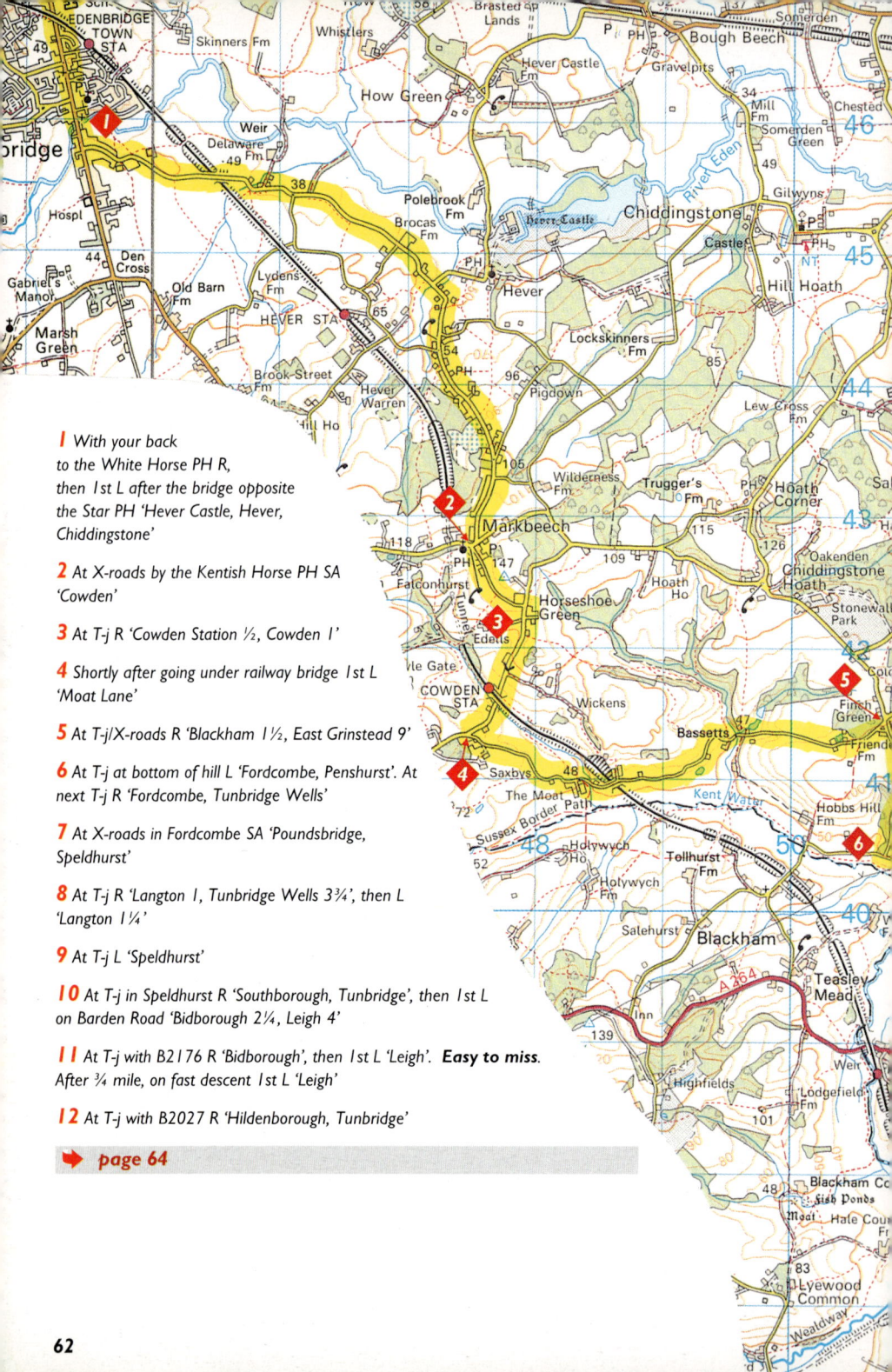

1 With your back
to the White Horse PH R,
then 1st L after the bridge opposite
the Star PH 'Hever Castle, Hever,
Chiddingstone'

2 At X-roads by the Kentish Horse PH SA
'Cowden'

3 At T-j R 'Cowden Station ½, Cowden 1'

4 Shortly after going under railway bridge 1st L
'Moat Lane'

5 At T-j/X-roads R 'Blackham 1½, East Grinstead 9'

6 At T-j at bottom of hill L 'Fordcombe, Penshurst'. At
next T-j R 'Fordcombe, Tunbridge Wells'

7 At X-roads in Fordcombe SA 'Poundsbridge,
Speldhurst'

8 At T-j R 'Langton 1, Tunbridge Wells 3¾', then L
'Langton 1¼'

9 At T-j L 'Speldhurst'

10 At T-j in Speldhurst R 'Southborough, Tunbridge', then 1st L
on Barden Road 'Bidborough 2¼, Leigh 4'

11 At T-j with B2176 R 'Bidborough', then 1st L 'Leigh'. **Easy to miss.**
After ¾ mile, on fast descent 1st L 'Leigh'

12 At T-j with B2027 R 'Hildenborough, Tunbridge'

➡ **page 64**

12 At T-j with B2027 R 'Hildenborough, Tunbridge'

13 Under the A21, then 1st L 'Sevenoaks (B245)'

14 After ¾ mile, at T-j with B245 L 'Sevenoaks', then R on Mill Lane

15 Follow signs for Underriver. Steep hill. As it levels 1st L on Fawke Wood Road 'River Hill 1½, Sevenoaks 3'

16 At T-j L 'Sevenoaks'

17 At T-j with A225 R, then 1st L on Gracious Lane 'Ide Hill 3'

18 At X-roads with Weald Road SA on continuation of Gracious Lane

19 After 1 mile, as road runs parallel with sunken A21 L on bridge over main road, then 1st R 'Ide Hill 2¼, Edenbridge 7'

20 At T-j with B2042 L (NS), then 1st R after sharp RH bend 'Ide Hill ¼, Sundridge 1½'

21 In Ide Hill follow roundabout to R, then 1st L immediately after National Trust Property Emmetts Garden

22 At T-j L 'Toys Hill ½ , Four Elms 2½, Edenbridge 5'. (If you are going to do route 7 as well leave the route here and follow the instructions on page 61)

23 At T-j with B2042 on sharp bend R (in effect SA) 'Four Elms ½, Edenbridge 3'. Busy stretch. At T-j in Edenbridge L to return to start

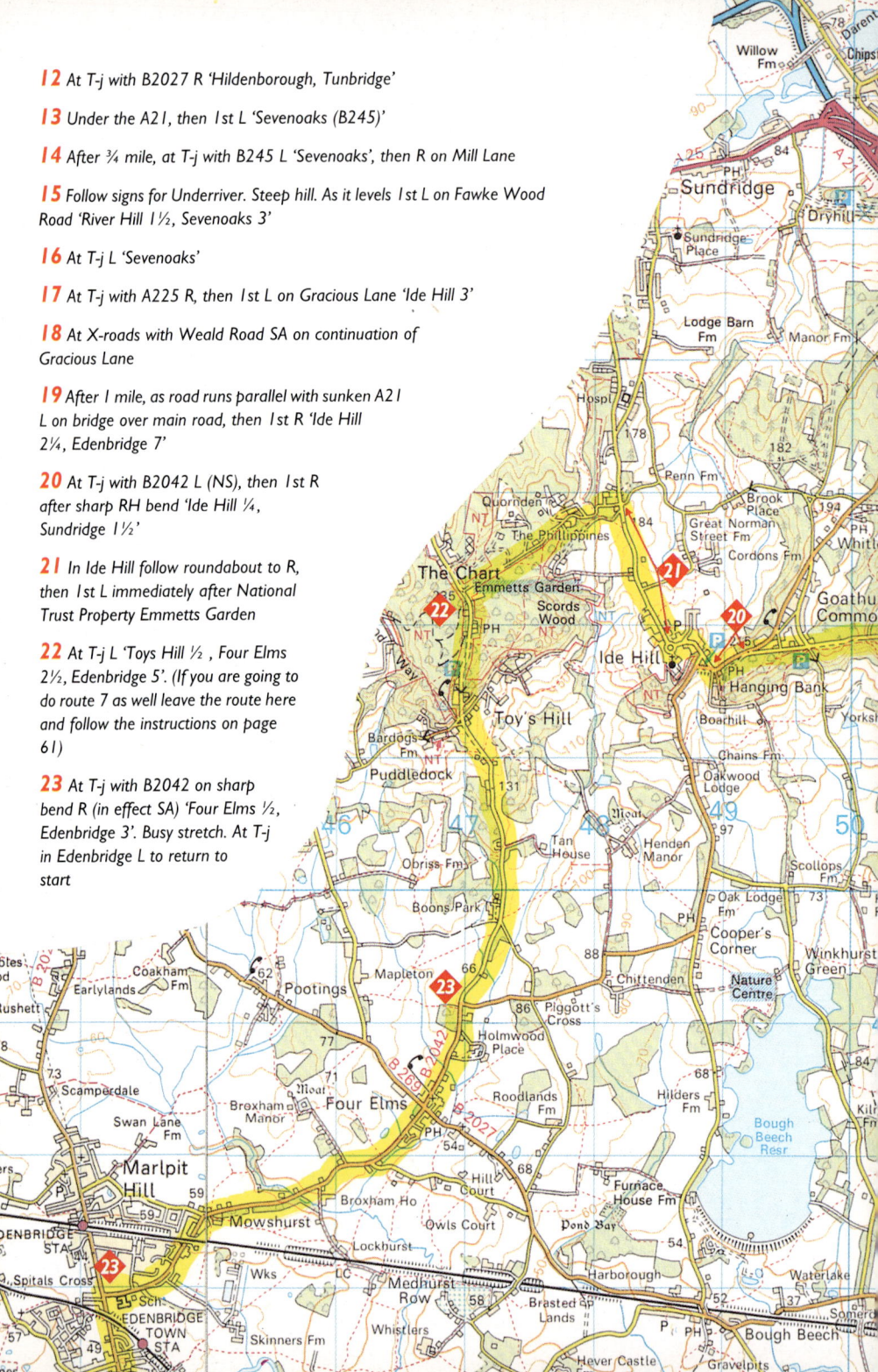

From Hailsham across the Pevensey Levels and over the Sussex Weald

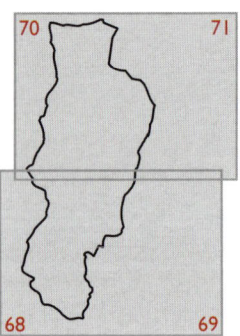

This ride dispels the idea that southeast England consists of two ranges of hills, the North and South Downs, with a flat section between called the Weald. The ride starts very gently across the Pevensey Levels, but north of Bodle Street Green the going gets tougher. This is a ride of small lanes and woodland, an exploration of the countryside with no specific focal point. Beautiful wooded stretches alternate with open views, and if you have any energy left you could always go for a swim at the leisure centre, where the ride starts and finishes.

Start

Leisure Centre, Hailsham

P As above

Distance and grade

33 miles

Moderate/strenuous

Terrain

From the flat Pevensey Levels to a very hilly middle section with four hills of over 300 feet and more than 2000 feet of climbing in total

Nearest railway

Polegate, 3 miles south of Hailsham, or Stonegate Station, 1½ miles north of the top northeast corner of the ride

Refreshments

Lots of choice in **Hailsham**
Welcome Stranger PH, **Windmill Hill**
White Horse PH ●, **Bodle Street Green**
Swan Inn ●●, **Wood's Corner**
Wheel PH ●, **Burwash Weald**
Kicking Donkey PH, **Witherenden Hill**
Star Inn ●●, **Old Heathfield**
Brewery Arms PH, **Vines Cross**

Hailsham

Golden Cross

Windmill Hill

Bodle Street Green

Wood's Corner

Michelham Priory, Upper Dicker (1-2)

West of Hailsham, slightly off the route, this priory was founded in 1229 but the moat and gatehouse were added in about 1400. After the Dissolution in 1536, the buildings were destroyed but were later repaired and incorporated into the Tudor house which stands here today. The priory rooms contain exhibitions illustrating the way of life of the Augustinian monks. The rooms in the Tudor section contain some of the original furniture and original oak beams can be seen in the kitchen.

Pevensey Castle (4)

Built by the Romans as a coastal fort and added to by the Normans, these are very impressive ruins. The chapel, keep and dungeon remain and some sections were refortified for use in the Second World War.

Herstmonceux Castle (6)

Beautifully restored in the early 20th century, this medieval castle is in very good condition. Built around a courtyard, there are octagonal towers on each corner and three other semi-octagonal ones. The imposing entrance has a gatehouse with portcullis and battlements. It is not open to the public but can be viewed by following the footpath and bridleway southeast of Herstmonceux church.

Burwash (13)

Standing on a ridge between rivers, this village was once a centre for iron-making and the 14th-century iron tomb-slab inside the Church of St Bartholomew is indicative of this. Timbered shops and cottages give character to the long main street.

Bateman's, Burwash (13)

The home of Rudyard Kipling from 1902 to 1936, this 17th-century house originally belonged to an ironmaster. Kipling's study remains as it was and some of his books and poems and his Rolls Royce are on display. A restored watermill grinds corn in the garden.

Horam Manor (21)

This manor has been the home of famous vintage cider makers since 1947 and there are guided tours and audio-visual presentations.

Burwash Common Great Bines Broad Oak Old Heathfield Vines Cross Grove Hill Hellingly

1 *From the leisure centre L. At T-j with High Street R, then L onto George Street, staying in LH lane 'Eastbourne A295'*

2 *Opposite The Terminus PH L on Station Road 'Station Road Industrial Estate'*

3 *After 1½ miles, on sharp RH bend by small circle of grass L (NS)*

4 Easy to miss. *After 2 miles, just before a long, low flint wall near a series of barns L 'Herstmonceux'*

5 *At T-j R 'Herstmonceux Castle and Church'. After ½ mile, opposite letter box 1st L 'Flowers Green' (Herstmonceux Castle is **not** open to the public)*

6 *At T-J in Flowers Green L (NS)*

7 *At T-j with A271 R 'Windmill Hill ½', then 1st L by petrol station on Victoria Road 'Bodle Street Green 1¾, Rushlake Green 5, Woods Corner 5'*

8 *After 2 miles at White Horse PH in Bodle Street Green R 'Woods Corner 3½'*

➡ **page 71**

22 *After 4 miles at T-j with A271 R 'Eastbourne', then L on Hawks Road 'Hailsham I'*

23 *At roundabout L 'Hailsham Industrial Estate'*

24 *In Hailsham shortly after traffic lights by Battle Road at beginning of one-way system L onto Vicarage Lane 'Leisure Centre and Lagoon'*

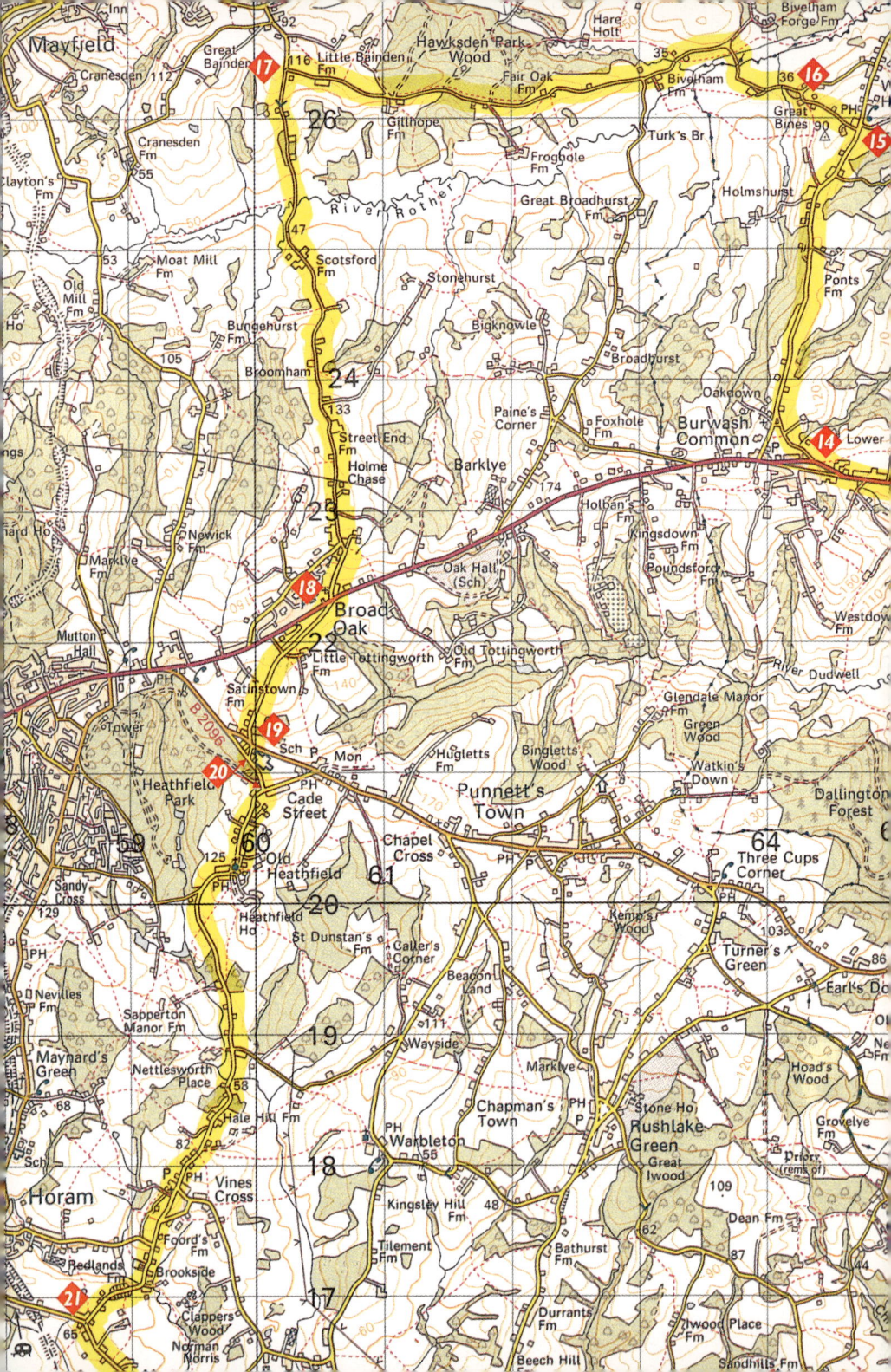

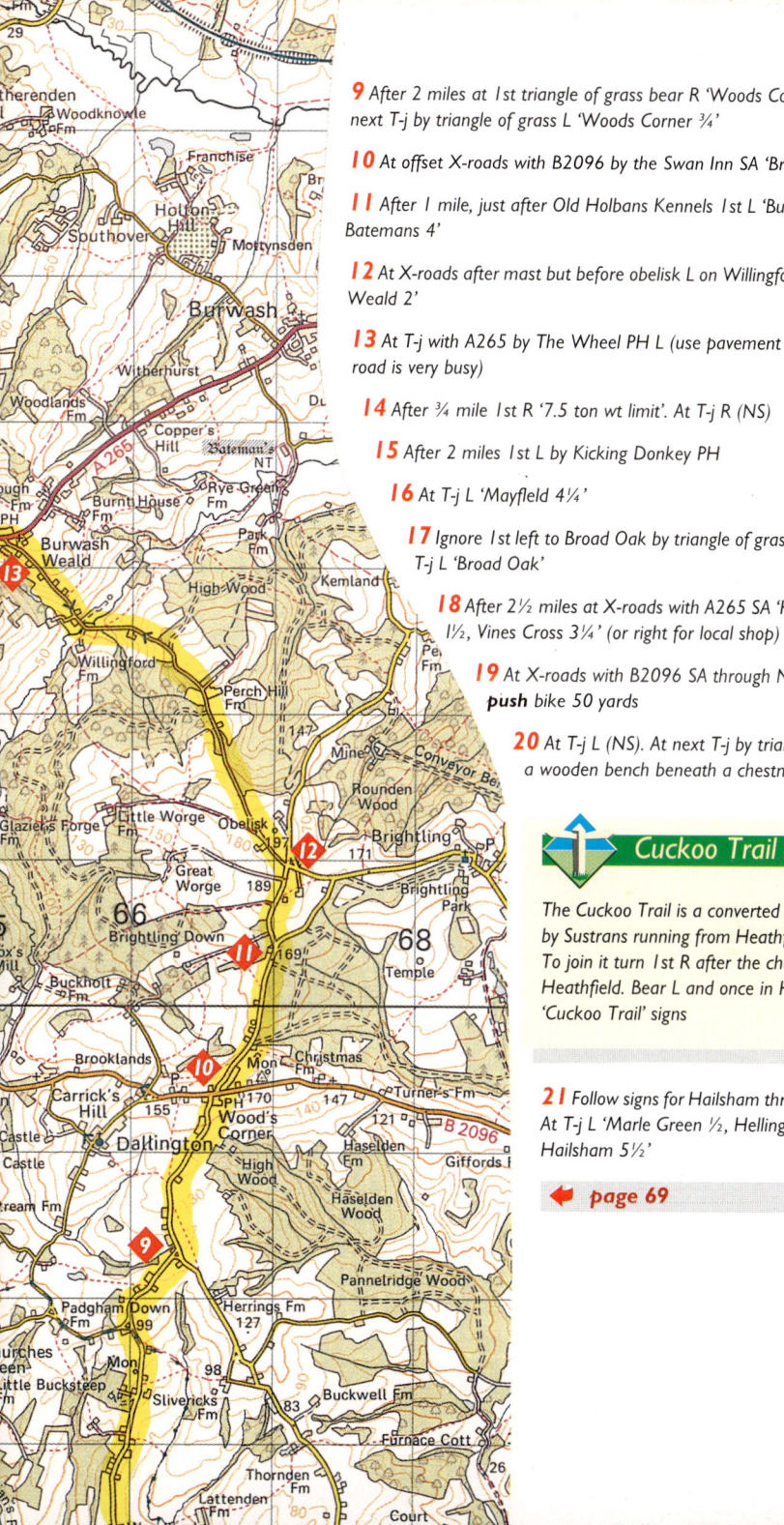

9 After 2 miles at 1st triangle of grass bear R 'Woods Corner'. Shortly, at next T-j by triangle of grass L 'Woods Corner ¾'

10 At offset X-roads with B2096 by the Swan Inn SA 'Brightling 1¾'

11 After 1 mile, just after Old Holbans Kennels 1st L 'Burwash 3, Batemans 4'

12 At X-roads after mast but before obelisk L on Willingford Lane 'Burwash Weald 2'

13 At T-j with A265 by The Wheel PH L (use pavement on far side if the road is very busy)

14 After ¾ mile 1st R '7.5 ton wt limit'. At T-j R (NS)

15 After 2 miles 1st L by Kicking Donkey PH

16 At T-j L 'Mayfield 4¼'

17 Ignore 1st left to Broad Oak by triangle of grass. After 3 miles at T-j L 'Broad Oak'

18 After 2½ miles at X-roads with A265 SA 'Heathfield Church 1½, Vines Cross 3¼' (or right for local shop)

19 At X-roads with B2096 SA through No Entry sign and **push** bike 50 yards

20 At T-j L (NS). At next T-j by triangle of grass with a wooden bench beneath a chestnut tree R (NS)

Cuckoo Trail alternative

The Cuckoo Trail is a converted railway path built by Sustrans running from Heathfield to Hailsham. To join it turn 1st R after the church in Old Heathfield. Bear L and once in Heathfield follow 'Cuckoo Trail' signs

21 Follow signs for Hailsham through Vines Cross. At T-j L 'Marle Green ½, Hellingly Hospital 3¾, Hailsham 5½'

← **page 69**

10 *Tenterden to Sissinghurst Castle*

A satisfying ride that takes in points of interest such as Sissinghurst Castle and the windmill at Woodchurch, the attractive villages of Headcorn, Smarden and Pluckley, some good pubs and wonderful scenery. Although the road between Tenterden and Sissinghurst is at times busy, this is soon forgotten as you turn off towards the old-world beauty of Sissinghurst Castle. The bridlepath that takes you through the estate may at times be a little rough but this diversion from the main road and past such a magnificent property is fine compensation for any slight discomfort. The ride can easily be shortened or it can be linked to Route 11, to form a 60-mile loop. (If you are doing the longer route, it is best to start with this ride and link it to Route 11 south of Wood-church at instruction 3.)

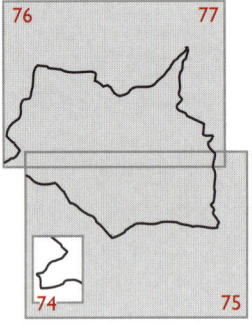

Start

Tourist Information Centre, Tenterden

P Follow signs

Distance and grade

33 miles

Easy/moderate

Terrain

Fairly flat or gentle, undulating hills. One climb worth noting: 270 feet between Smarden and Pluckley

Nearest railway

Pluckley

Refreshments

Lots of choice in **Tenterden**
Bull Inn 🍴, **Sissinghurst**
Coffee and teas at **Sissinghurst Castle**
Bell and Jorrods PH, **Frittenden**
Kings Arms PH, George and Dragon PH 🍴, **Headcorn**
The Bell PH 🍴🍴, Smarden Bell PH,
Chequers PH 🍴, **Smarden**
Black Horse PH 🍴, **Pluckley**
Dering Arms PH 🍴🍴, **Pluckley Station**
Bonny Cravat PH, Six Bells PH, **Woodchurch**

Tenterden Parkgate Fosten Green Golford Sissinghurst Sissinghurst Castle Frittenden Headcorn

Sissinghurst Garden (3)
These gardens were created by Vita Sackville West and her husband Sir Harold Nicholson in the 1930s. A series of small gardens are enclosed within the remains of an Elizabethan mansion.

Headcorn Flower Centre and Vineyard (7–8)
Award-winning wine is produced at this vineyard and can be tasted free of charge at the end of a visit. Chrysanthemums and orchid lilies bloom all year round in the flower houses and there is a large reservoir stocked with trout.

Smarden (10)
This an old wool village with an Elizabethan market place and many interesting old buildings. The large parish church has a copy of an Elizabethan charter granting permission for a weekly market and an annual fair.

Woodchurch Windmill (14–15)
This restored smock mill, now in working order, contains an exhibition charting the mill's history.

Rare Breeds Centre, Woodchurch (15)
90 acres of farmland house this important collection of rare animals. There is a 'kiddies corner' where many young animals can be handled.

Tenterden (16–17)
The name Tenterden comes from the earliest settlement: a pig pasture for the men of Thanet. By the 14th century, sheep were the main source of wealth and a flourishing cloth industry developed. Tenterden prospered and became a member of the Confederation of the Cinque Ports. St Mildred's Church dominates the main street with its impressive pinnacled tower built in the 15th century of Bethersden marble. The 13th-century chancel is the oldest section of the church and has an Early English lancet window with a modern stained glass representation of St Mildred. The Woolpack Inn and the Tudor Rose date from the 15th century and, unlike some other buildings in the High Street (such as the Eight Bells Inn), have not been given 18th- or 19th-century facades.

The Tenterden and District Museum (17)
This explains the town's interesting history and also houses a railway museum. The main station nearby was closed in 1954 but now runs steam train trips into the Wealden countryside.

Maltman's Hill   Pluckley   Bethersden   Brissenden Green   Shirkoak   Woodchurch   Brook Street

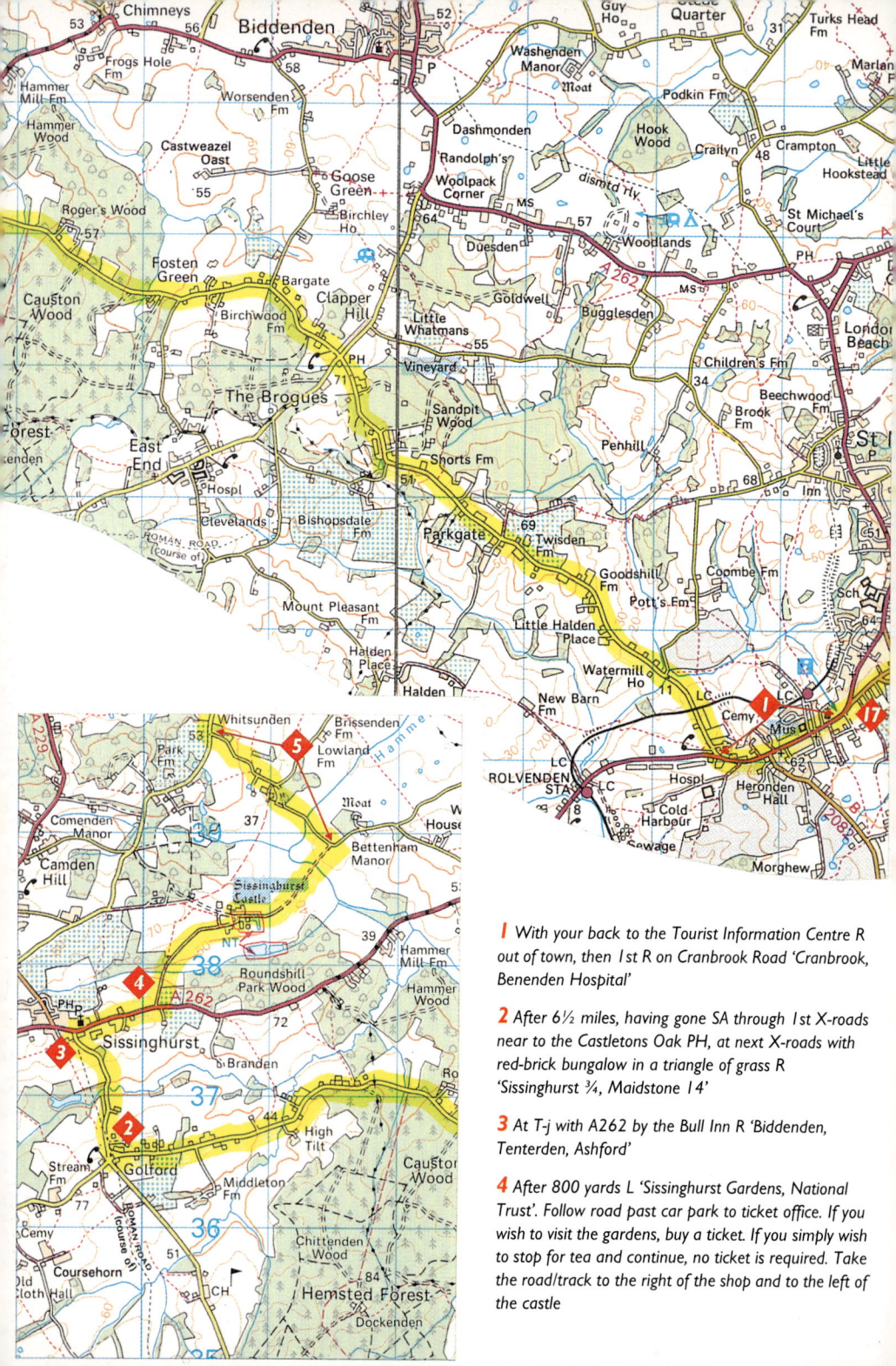

1 With your back to the Tourist Information Centre R out of town, then 1st R on Cranbrook Road 'Cranbrook, Benenden Hospital'

2 After 6½ miles, having gone SA through 1st X-roads near to the Castletons Oak PH, at next X-roads with red-brick bungalow in a triangle of grass R 'Sissinghurst ¾, Maidstone 14'

3 At T-j with A262 by the Bull Inn R 'Biddenden, Tenterden, Ashford'

4 After 800 yards L 'Sissinghurst Gardens, National Trust'. Follow road past car park to ticket office. If you wish to visit the gardens, buy a ticket. If you simply wish to stop for tea and continue, no ticket is required. Take the road/track to the right of the shop and to the left of the castle

6 Through Frittenden, following signs for Headcorn. At T-j R 'Headcorn ¼, Lenham 7'

7 At X-roads with A274 R on North Street 'Biddenden, Tenterden'

8 On sharp RH bend at end of village L 'Smarden'

9 At T-j by The Bell PH L 'Smarden', then 1st R 'Smarden'

10 In Smarden at T-j by Chequers PH L

11 After 3½ miles, in Pluckley at top of the hill R 'Bethersden'

12 After 3½ miles you will pass a timber frame works. At X-roads SA 'Great Chart, Ashford', then 1st R on Kiln Lane

13 At T-j with A28 L (NS), then after ½ mile 1st R ' Woodchurch 4'

← **page 75**

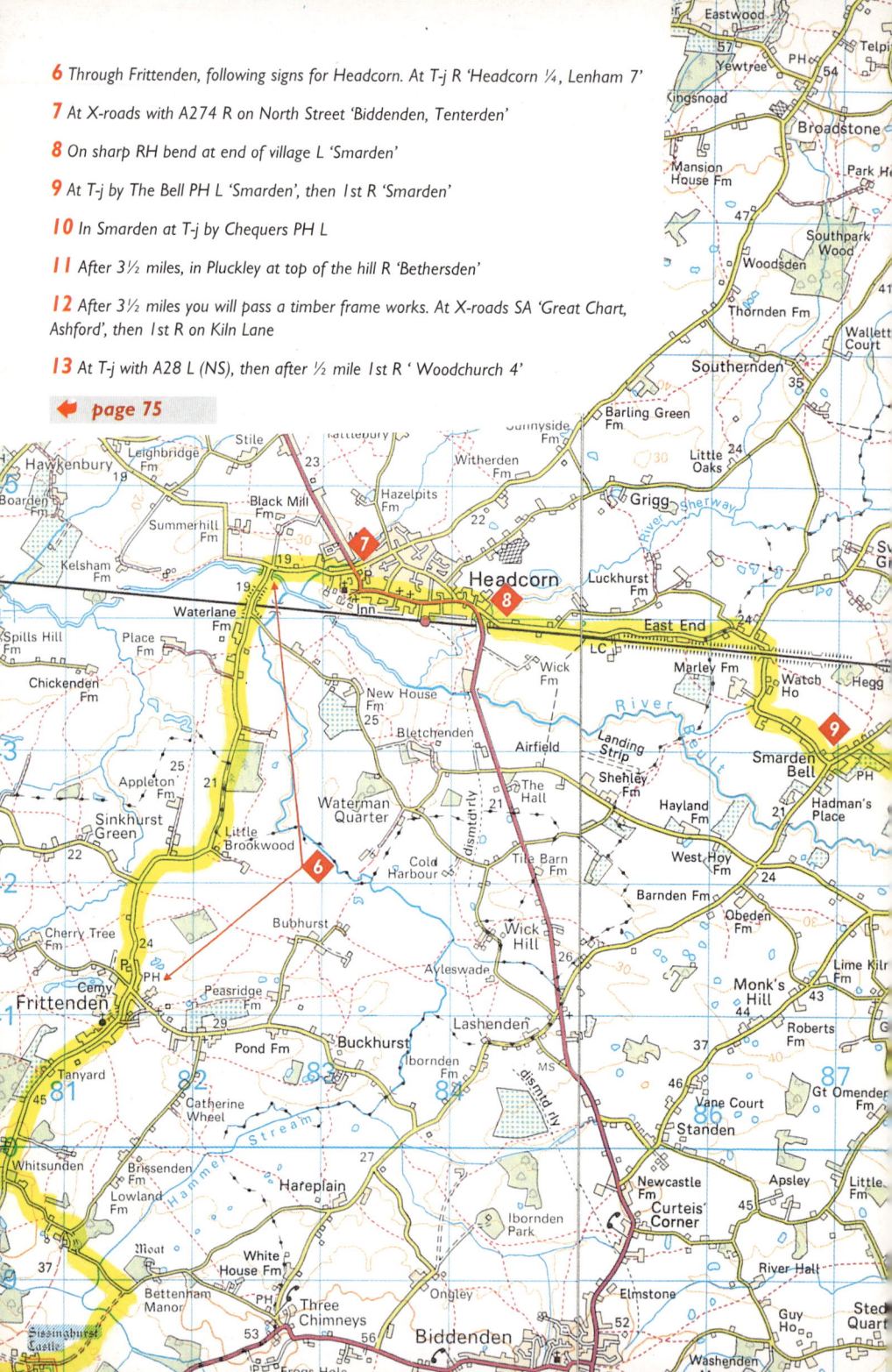

5 *The bridletrack becomes rougher and crosses a bridge over a stream. At the road L, then at T-j R 'Frittenden 1, Headcorn 4'*

➡ **page 76**

14 *Follow signs for Woodchurch, past the windmill and through the village*

15 *At T-j with B2067 R 'Tenterden'. (To link with Ride 11 turn 1st L after ¾ mile and join at instructions nos. 3 & 4, page 81)*

16 *At X-roads SA 'Town Centre'*

17 *At T-j R (NS), then at T-j by traffic lights L back to the start*

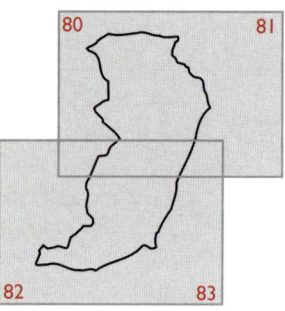

South from Tenterden to Rye

Start

Tourist Information Centre, Tenterden

P Follow signs

Distance and grade

33 miles

🌿 Easy

Terrain

From the very flat to the gently undulating. Two hills of 200 feet, west of Rye then north of Udimore

Nearest railway

Appledore or Rye

An easy ride through the flat moors and marshes of west Kent and East Sussex. The lane across Shirley Moor is a real delight, with a refreshment stop at Appledore to look forward to. A straight section alongside the Military Canal leads to the charms of Rye, one of the Cinque Ports. Two gentle climbs west then north through woodlands drop you back on the levels at the bridge over the Otter Channel. This ride can easily be linked to Route 10, north from Tenterden to Sissinghurst and Pluckley, to form a 60-mile loop.

Refreshments

Lots of choice in **Tenterden**
Red Lion PH, Swan PH, Sentry Box Tea Rooms, **Appledore**
Mermaid PH 🍴🍴, lots of choice in **Rye**
Bull Inn, Kings Head PH **Udimore**
Coffee and tea at Flackley Ash Hotel, **Peasmarsh**
Ewe and Lambs PH, **Wittersham**
Wine and ale bar, wine tasting, tea and coffee at
Tenterden Vineyards, Small Hythe

Tenterden   Brook Street   Appledore Heath   Appledore   Stone Bridge   Scot's Float   Rye

Appledore (5)

Originally on the coast, Appledore was an important ship-building centre. During the Napeolonic Wars, the Royal Military Canal was constructed and a short section of it is now preserved by the National Trust. In the village are many interesting buildings from various periods.

Rye

Rye (6-7)

This beautiful hilltop town has had a turbulent history: it was partially destroyed by the sea in the 14th century, frequently attacked by the French and nearly burned down in 1377. It enjoyed privileged status as a Cinque Port town and was an important trading point with merchants, pirates and smugglers. Although the sea has retreated, the town is still surrounded by three rivers and has well-preserved 16th-century timbered houses, 18th-century winding cobbled streets and many places of interest including:

The Landgate

Built by Edward III in 1329, this gateway was the only means of entering the town at high tide.

Mermaid Inn

This inn was founded in the 11th century and became the headquarters for an infamous smuggling gang. Mermaid Street is one of the prettiest in Rye.

Ypres Tower

This tower is one of the oldest surviving buildings in Rye; it was built in 1250 to protect the town from the French.

Rye Town Model Sound and Light Show

An excellent way of hearing the story of Rye, this show combines dramatic light and sound effects with a model of the town.

Small Hythe (14-1)

Smallhythe Place is an early 16th-century house that was originally a port house and shipyard; it later belonged to the actress Dame Ellen Terry and now contains displays of theatrical memorabilia. Nearby are the Tenterden Vineyards where the winery and processing equipment can be seen and then the wine tasted; there is also a large herb garden.

The Hermitage   Peasmarsh   Wittersham   Peening Quarter   Small Hythe

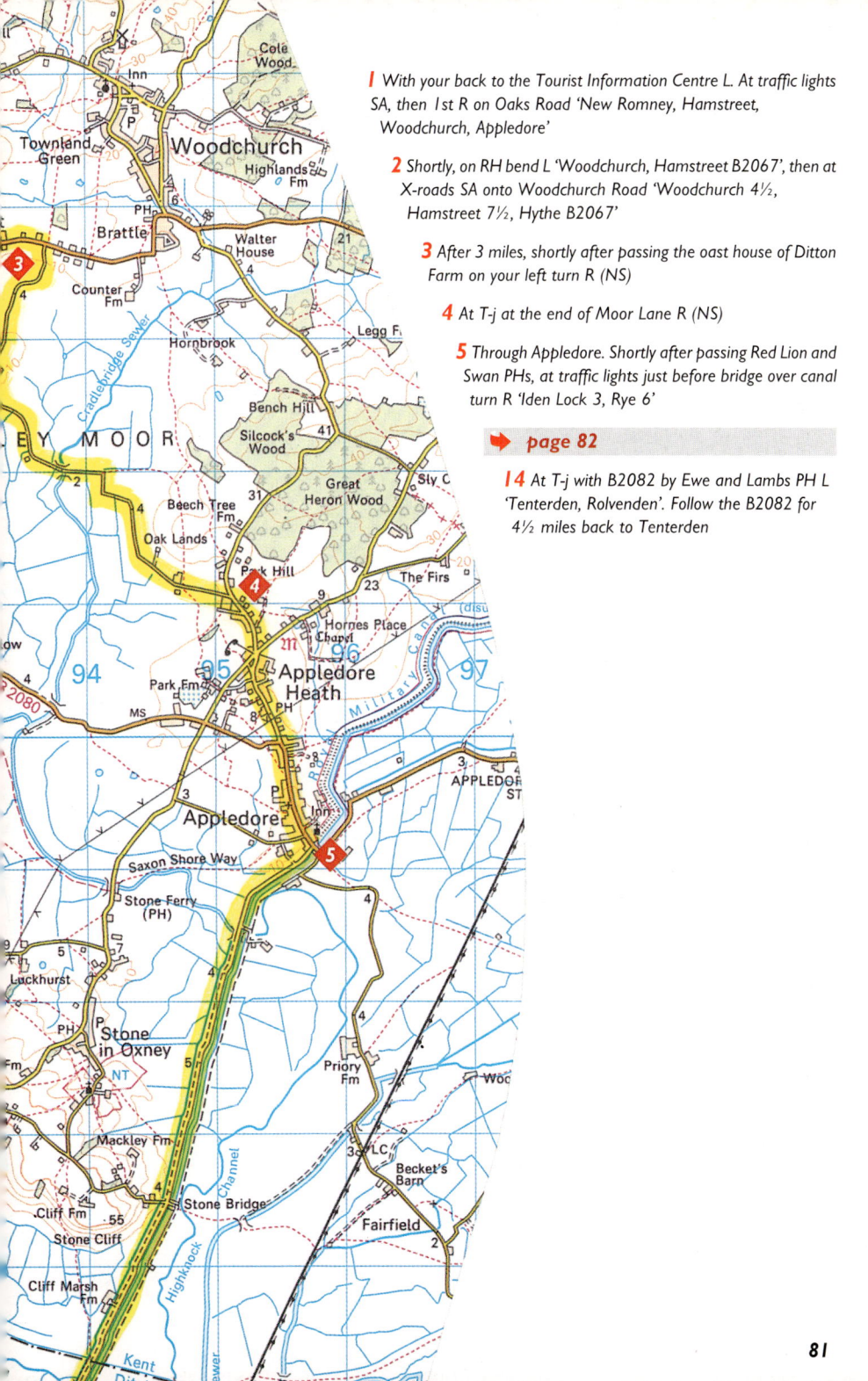

1 With your back to the Tourist Information Centre L. At traffic lights SA, then 1st R on Oaks Road 'New Romney, Hamstreet, Woodchurch, Appledore'

2 Shortly, on RH bend L 'Woodchurch, Hamstreet B2067', then at X-roads SA onto Woodchurch Road 'Woodchurch 4½, Hamstreet 7½, Hythe B2067'

3 After 3 miles, shortly after passing the oast house of Ditton Farm on your left turn R (NS)

4 At T-j at the end of Moor Lane R (NS)

5 Through Appledore. Shortly after passing Red Lion and Swan PHs, at traffic lights just before bridge over canal turn R 'Iden Lock 3, Rye 6'

➡ **page 82**

14 At T-j with B2082 by Ewe and Lambs PH L 'Tenterden, Rolvenden'. Follow the B2082 for 4½ miles back to Tenterden

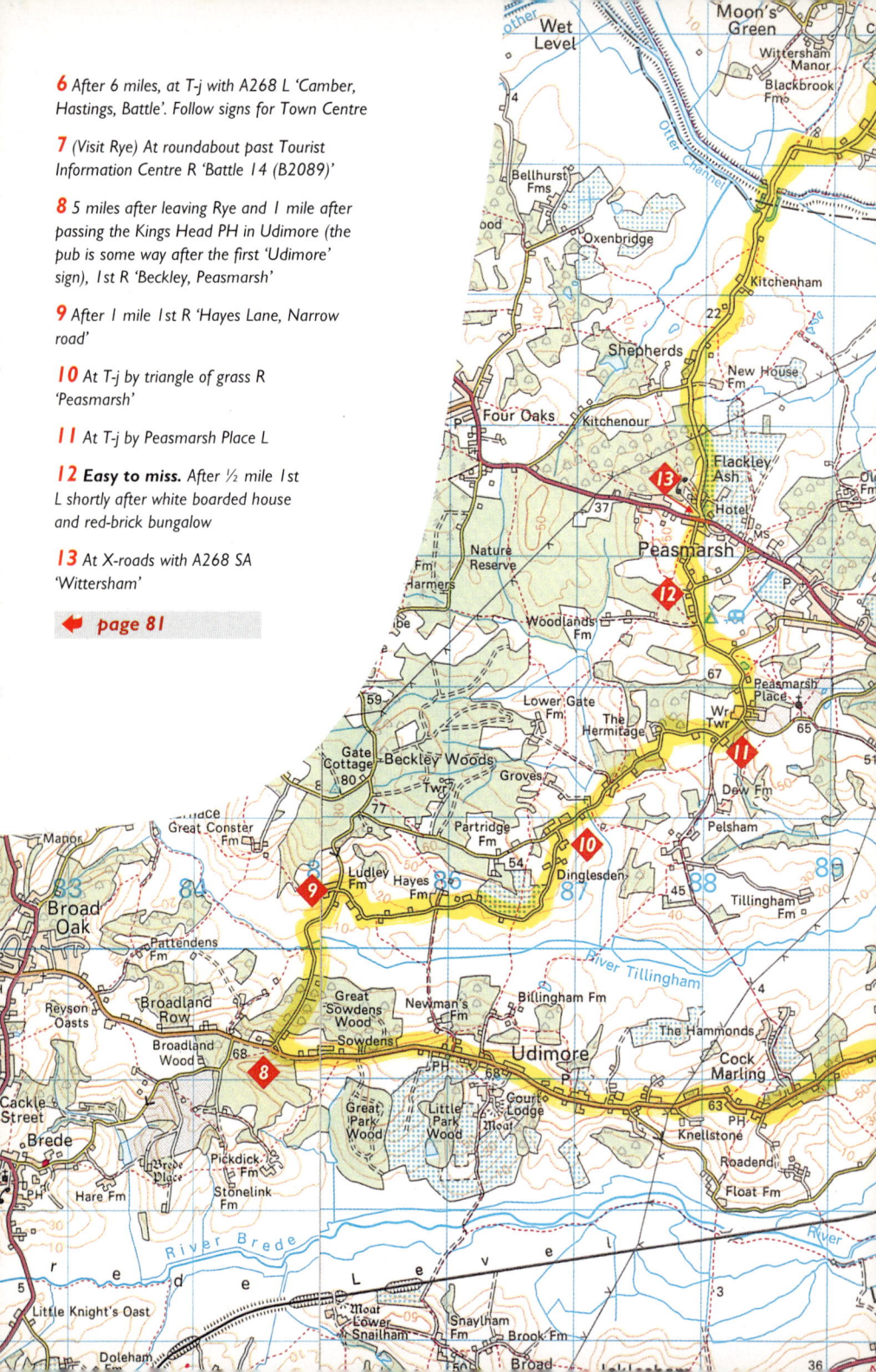

6 After 6 miles, at T-j with A268 L 'Camber, Hastings, Battle'. Follow signs for Town Centre

7 (Visit Rye) At roundabout past Tourist Information Centre R 'Battle 14 (B2089)'

8 5 miles after leaving Rye and 1 mile after passing the Kings Head PH in Udimore (the pub is some way after the first 'Udimore' sign), 1st R 'Beckley, Peasmarsh'

9 After 1 mile 1st R 'Hayes Lane, Narrow road'

10 At T-j by triangle of grass R 'Peasmarsh'

11 At T-j by Peasmarsh Place L

12 **Easy to miss.** After ½ mile 1st L shortly after white boarded house and red-brick bungalow

13 At X-roads with A268 SA 'Wittersham'

← **page 81**

12 *Wye to Chilham*

As with Route 13 that starts in Wye, this ride features lots of stretches of beautiful lanes linked together in an exploration of the rolling downland between the A20/M20 and the A2/M2. The scenery is typical of Kent, with many oast houses, orchards and fields of hops. The village of Chilham is a real delight with pubs, tea shops and a castle to visit. The ride finishes with some lovely wooded lanes through Sole Street and Crundale.

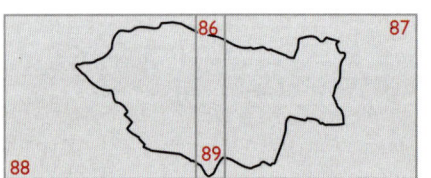

Start

The church in Wye

P Follow signs to free parking near start

Distance and grade

32 miles

Moderate

Terrain

Two climbs of 400 feet – between Westwell and Charing Hill and between Shalmsford Street and Sole Street. Several short, steep hills, The Wynd just north of Charing is fiercesome!

Nearest railway

Wye

Refreshments

New Flying Horse PH, Tickled Trout PH, **Wye**
Flying Horse PH, **Boughton Lees**
Wheel Inn, **Westwell**
Bowl Inn, **north of Charing Hill**
The Plough PH, **Shottenden**
White Horse PH, Woolpack PH,
tea shops, **Chilham**
Ye Olde England PH, **Shalmsford Street**
Compasses PH, **Sole Street**

Wye   Boughton Lees   Westwell   Charing Hill   Warren Street   Yewhedges   Hockley

Wye (1)

There are good views across the Stour Valley from this unspoilt market town. The Church of St Gregory and St Martin houses some interesting collections. Also interesting is Wye College, founded in the 15th century by John Kempe (who later became Archbishop of Canterbury) and now an agricultural college.

Chilham Castle

Agricultural Museum, Brook (1)

Slightly off the route, a wide collection of farm implements is displayed in a 14th-century tithe barn and a 19th-century oast house.

Doddington Place Gardens (4)

Beautiful rhododendrons and azaleas, a sunken garden, a rock garden and expansive lawns can be found within these 10 acres of landscaped garden.

Chilham (20-21)

The village grew up around the gates of the medieval castle. The central square is dominated by St Mary's Church and narrow streets full of pretty cottages lead off from this.

Chilham Castle (20)

Only the octagonal keep remains of the original Norman castle; the present castle was completed in 1616 and stands between the medieval ruins and the village and is not open to the public. The large gardens contain a lake, a rose garden, a deer park and a 'petland' for children.

Shottenden   Chilham   Old Wives Lees   Shalmsford Street   Denge Wood   Sole Street   Olantigh

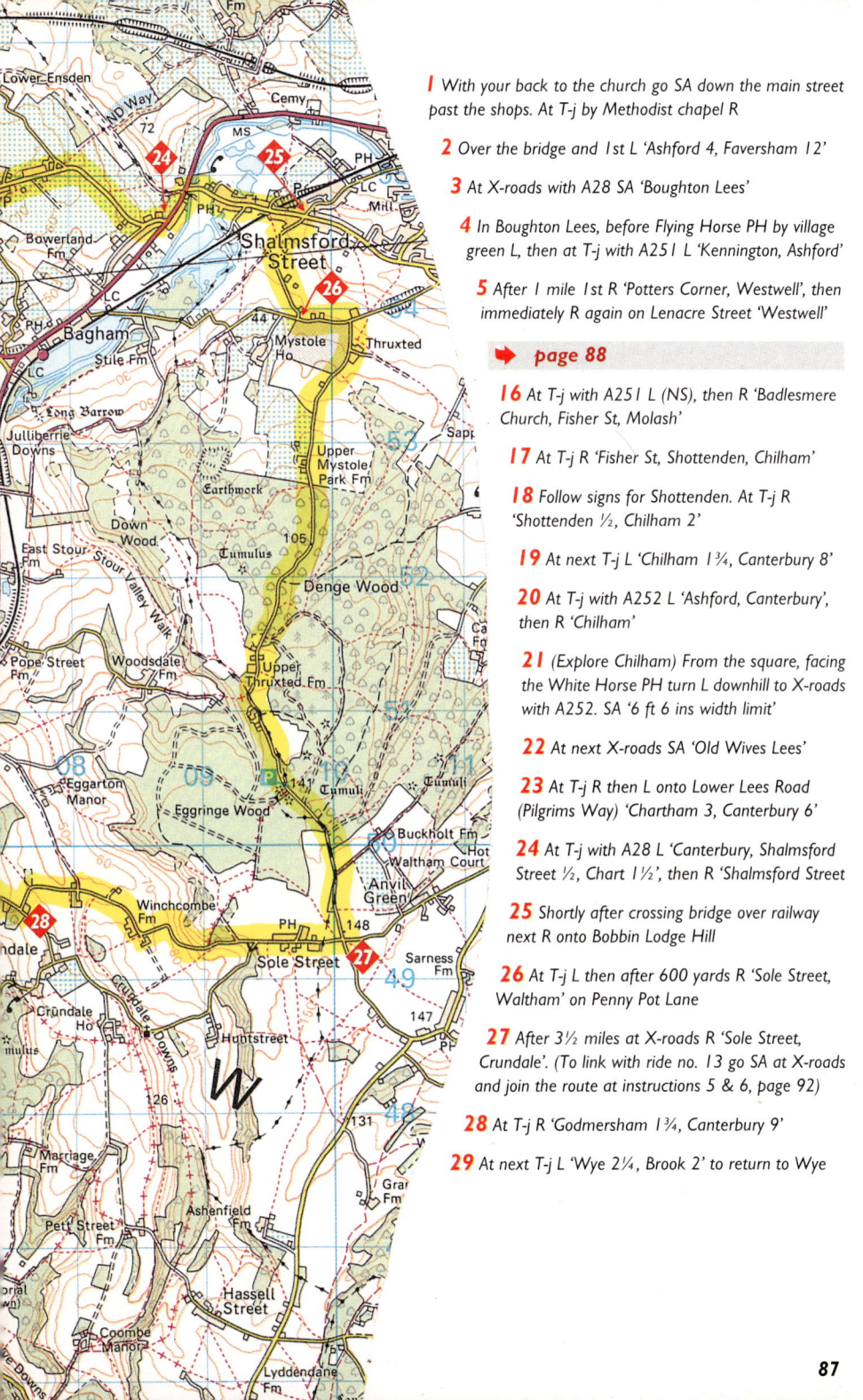

1 With your back to the church go SA down the main street past the shops. At T-j by Methodist chapel R

2 Over the bridge and 1st L 'Ashford 4, Faversham 12'

3 At X-roads with A28 SA 'Boughton Lees'

4 In Boughton Lees, before Flying Horse PH by village green L, then at T-j with A251 L 'Kennington, Ashford'

5 After 1 mile 1st R 'Potters Corner, Westwell', then immediately R again on Lenacre Street 'Westwell'

➡ **page 88**

16 At T-j with A251 L (NS), then R 'Badlesmere Church, Fisher St, Molash'

17 At T-j R 'Fisher St, Shottenden, Chilham'

18 Follow signs for Shottenden. At T-j R 'Shottenden ½, Chilham 2'

19 At next T-j L 'Chilham 1¾, Canterbury 8'

20 At T-j with A252 L 'Ashford, Canterbury', then R 'Chilham'

21 (Explore Chilham) From the square, facing the White Horse PH turn L downhill to X-roads with A252. SA '6 ft 6 ins width limit'

22 At next X-roads SA 'Old Wives Lees'

23 At T-j R then L onto Lower Lees Road (Pilgrims Way) 'Chartham 3, Canterbury 6'

24 At T-j with A28 L 'Canterbury, Shalmsford Street ½, Chart 1½', then R 'Shalmsford Street

25 Shortly after crossing bridge over railway next R onto Bobbin Lodge Hill

26 At T-j L then after 600 yards R 'Sole Street, Waltham' on Penny Pot Lane

27 After 3½ miles at X-roads R 'Sole Street, Crundale'. (To link with ride no. 13 go SA at X-roads and join the route at instructions 5 & 6, page 92)

28 At T-j R 'Godmersham 1¾, Canterbury 9'

29 At next T-j L 'Wye 2¼, Brook 2' to return to Wye

4 In Boughton Lees, before Flying Horse PH by village green L, then at T-j with A251 L 'Kennington, Ashford'

5 After 1 mile 1st R 'Potters Corner, Westwell', then immediately R again on Lenacre Street 'Westwell'

6 In Westwell at offset X-roads SA 'Charing 3¾, Maidstone 16¼'

7 After 1 mile 2nd R on LH bend just after large red-brick house 'Charing'

8 At T-j after 1½ miles R (NS)

9 At T-j with A252 at the end of Pett Lane R, then 1st L on The Wynd (very steep), then at T-j L

10 At X-roads near Bowl Inn PH SA 'Warren Street 2, Lenham 4'

11 At T-j at end of Wareditch Road R 'Stalisfield 2¾'

12 After 3 miles, shortly after passing, on your left, a turning to Newnham and Doddington by a large oak tree and then Wingfield Farm take next R (NS)

13 At T-j R 'Throwley, Sheldwich'

14 At T-j L 'Throwley 1¼, Sheldwich 3, Faversham 5', then 1st R 'Belmont ¾, Throwley 1, Sheldwich 2'

15 After ¾ mile, on sharp RH bend L 'Badlesmere, Sheldwich'

16 At T-j with A251 L (NS), then R 'Badlesmere Church, Fisher St, Molash'

17 At T-j R 'Fisher St, Shottenden, Chilham'

← **page 87**

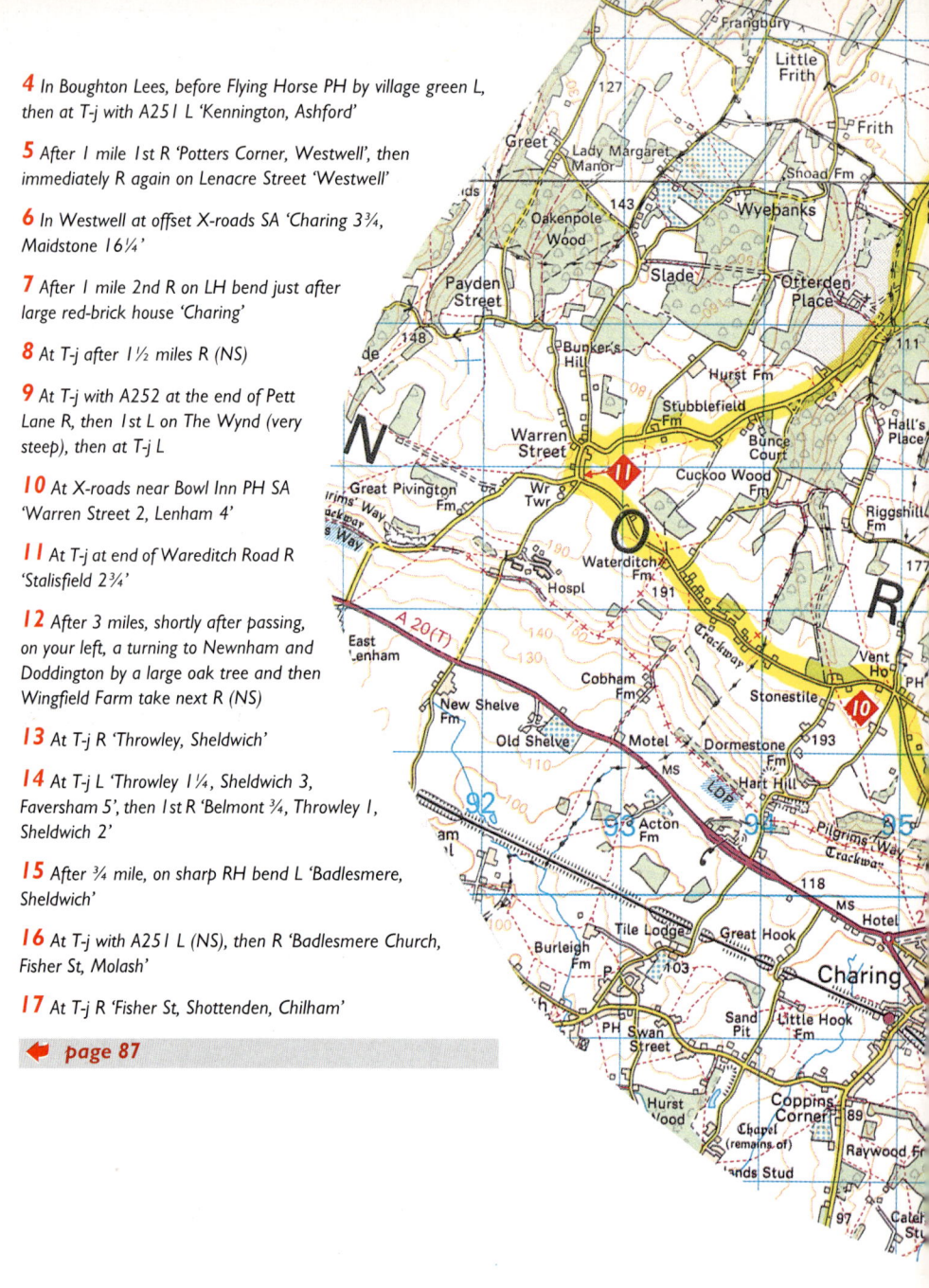

13 Narrow lanes and extensive views on the eastern end of the North Downs

This is a Chinese puzzle of a ride with as many instructions as there are miles covered. It links together short sections of beautiful, wooded, steep twisting lanes at the eastern end of the North Downs. The whole area is a maze of little lanes, ideal for exploration by bike if you are not in a pressing hurry to get from A to B. There are many points along the ride with good views, but the best are from Farthing Common with the downs spreading away to the northwest and the English Channel to the south.

Start

The church in Wye

 P Follow signs to free parking close to the start

Distance and grade

32 miles

Moderate/strenuous

Terrain

Although there is only one climb of over 300 feet, this ride seems very hilly with lots of short, sharp climbs, at times as steep as 1:4

Nearest railway

Wye

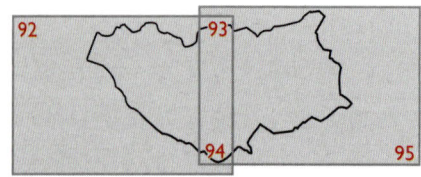

Refreshments

Tickled Trout PH, New Flying Horse PH, tea shops, **Wye**
Compasses PH, **Sole Street**
Lord Nelson PH, **Waltham**
Star Inn, **Bossingham**
Duke of Cumberland PH, **Barham**
Jackdaw PH, **Denton**
Endeavour PH, **Wootton**
Coach and Horses PH, **Lyminge**
Tiger Inn, **Stowting**

Wye Crundale Sole Street Waltham Bossingham Barham Gravel Castle Lodge Lees Denton

Parsonage Farm Rural Heritage Centre (23)
The history of domestic animals is displayed at this farm and there are many rare and traditional breeds to be seen. A small exhibition tells the story of the farm.

Lyminge (24)
Most of Lyminge is Victorian but its history begins in 633 when King Ethelbert's daughter and Bishop Paulinus founded an abbey here. Some of the original walls were incorporated into the village church.

Saltwood Castle (26)
Slightly off the route, this castle was probably built by a Warden of the Cinque Ports in 1160. It is said that the four knights who murdered Thomas Becket in 1170 stayed over night here on their way to Canterbury. By the 14th century, the inner bailey walls and towers were completed and in the 1380s the Archbishop William Courtenay added the triangular outer bailey, the gatehouse to the inner bailey, inscribed with his arms, and some domestic buildings. Much was damaged in an earthquake in 1580 but some parts have been well restored.

Wye Downs (31)
These form part of the North Downs and are covered in woodland and shrubs. The area is a nature reserve.

Swingfield Minnis

Acrise Place

Ottinge

Lyminge

Stowting Court

Amage Farm

1 With your back to the church, facing the main street L out of town, then 1st L on Olantigh Road by telephone box 'Crundale'

2 Shortly after passing stately manor house on left (Olantigh), at top of small hill turn R 'Olantigh Nurseries'

3 After 400 yards at triangle of grass L (sign broken)

4 In Crundale at bottom of hill on sharp LH bend R (in effect SA) 'Crundale Church 1½'

5 Steep hill. At T-j R (NS). At X-roads R 'Waltham, Hastingleigh'

6 At T-j at end of Richdore Road, by a triangle of grass L 'Petham 2¼, Canterbury 7', then 1st R by Lord Nelson PH onto Church Lane

7 At T-j R 'Elmsted 2, Hastingleigh 3, Ashford 10', then 1st L

8 At T-j with B2068 L (NS), then 1st R. At T-j R (NS)

➡ **page 95**

27 Views of the sea to the left. At T-j with B2068 R, then 1st L 'Monks Horton, Stowting'

28 At X-roads R 'Stowting, Brabourne'

29 After 1½ miles, at 4-way junction just before sign for Brabourne bear R (in effect SA) 'Brook, Wye'

30 After 1¼ miles, shortly after left turning to Brabourne, as road climbs escarpment L downhill 'Brook 3, Wye 2½'

31 At T-j by triangle of grass R 'Wye 1¾, Canterbury 13'

32 At T-j L 'Wye ½'

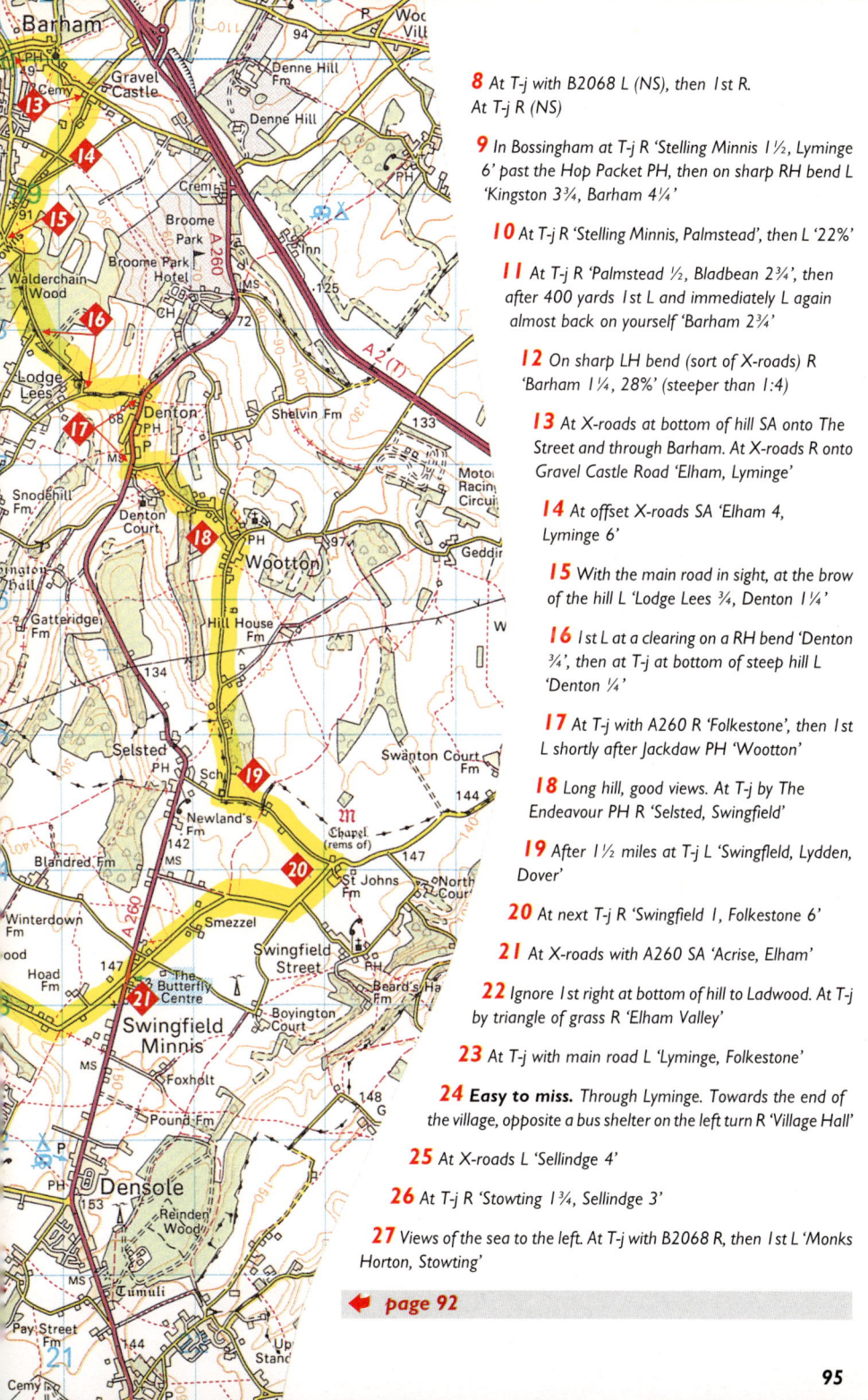

8 At T-j with B2068 L (NS), then 1st R. At T-j R (NS)

9 In Bossingham at T-j R 'Stelling Minnis 1½, Lyminge 6' past the Hop Packet PH, then on sharp RH bend L 'Kingston 3¾, Barham 4¼'

10 At T-j R 'Stelling Minnis, Palmstead', then L '22%'

11 At T-j R 'Palmstead ½, Bladbean 2¾', then after 400 yards 1st L and immediately L again almost back on yourself 'Barham 2¾'

12 On sharp LH bend (sort of X-roads) R 'Barham 1¼, 28%' (steeper than 1:4)

13 At X-roads at bottom of hill SA onto The Street and through Barham. At X-roads R onto Gravel Castle Road 'Elham, Lyminge'

14 At offset X-roads SA 'Elham 4, Lyminge 6'

15 With the main road in sight, at the brow of the hill L 'Lodge Lees ¾, Denton 1¼'

16 1st L at a clearing on a RH bend 'Denton ¾', then at T-j at bottom of steep hill L 'Denton ¼'

17 At T-j with A260 R 'Folkestone', then 1st L shortly after Jackdaw PH 'Wootton'

18 Long hill, good views. At T-j by The Endeavour PH R 'Selsted, Swingfield'

19 After 1½ miles at T-j L 'Swingfield, Lydden, Dover'

20 At next T-j R 'Swingfield 1, Folkestone 6'

21 At X-roads with A260 SA 'Acrise, Elham'

22 Ignore 1st right at bottom of hill to Ladwood. At T-j by triangle of grass R 'Elham Valley'

23 At T-j with main road L 'Lyminge, Folkestone'

24 **Easy to miss.** Through Lyminge. Towards the end of the village, opposite a bus shelter on the left turn R 'Village Hall'

25 At X-roads L 'Sellindge 4'

26 At T-j R 'Stowting 1¾, Sellindge 3'

27 Views of the sea to the left. At T-j with B2068 R, then 1st L 'Monks Horton, Stowting'

← **page 92**

14 *Sandwich and quiet Kent villages in the southeastern corner of England*

Start

Tourist Information Centre, Sandwich

P Follow signs

Distance and grade

32 miles

Easy

Terrain

Flat or undulating, no major climbs

Nearest railway

Sandwich, Bekesbourne Hill or Aylesham

Starting at Sandwich, one of the Cinque Ports and a very attractive old town, the ride takes in the gentle, rolling countryside of the eastern part of Kent. As the ride moves west, you start passing the orchards of fruit trees that give Kent its sobriquet 'The garden of England'. Next come the picturesque villages of Littlebourne and Wickhambreaux. The final stretch through Preston and Goldstone gives one the impression of being at the extremity of a country, even though the Isle of Thanet and Margate lie further east and north. Just before your return to Sandwich you pass the ruins of Richborough Castle.

98	99
100	101

Refreshments

Lots of choice in **Sandwich**
Hare and Hounds PH, **Northbourne**
Butchers Arms PH, **Studdal** Crown Inn, **Eythorne**
White Horse PH, **Lower Eythorne**
Yew Tree PH, **Barfrestone**
Bulls Head PH, **Adisham**
King William IV PH, The Anchor PH, **Littlebourne**
Rose Inn ●, **Wickhambreaux**
Half Moon PH, **Preston**

Sandwich — Ham — Northbourne — Sutton — East Studdal — Ashley — Eythorne / Lower Eythorne — Barfrestone / Frogham — Ratling

Sandwich (1)

Sandwich is an excellently preserved medieval town with many interesting buildings. It was one of the original Cinque Ports when the Confederation was formed by Edward the Confessor in 1050. In return for many privileges, these towns provided ships and the men to work on them.

Guildhall (1)

Built during the reign of Elizabeth I, the Guildhall has since been modified but still has many interesting historical and architectural features. An oak screen dating from 1300 is on display in the Courtroom.

The Butts (1)

The original town wall was built in 1384 and part of it remains.

Strand Street (1)

Many of the town's oldest buildings are on this street: St Mary's Church was built on the site of a Saxon Nunnery by the Normans; the 'Sandwich Weavers' was used as a workshop and home by 16th-century Dutch refugees; 'The Pilgrims' are 14th-century merchant houses with overhanging upper floors.

Northbourne Court (5-6)

This garden has Saxon origins but its terraced structure is Jacobean. It consists of several small gardens enclosed by high walls and there is great character shown in the unusual selection of plants.

Goodnestone Park Gardens, near Wingham (15)

A large garden, surrounded by parkland, with formal terraces and some unusual plants and trees. Jane Austen visited many times.

Howletts Zoo Park, Bekesbourne (17-18)

Specializing in breeding rare animals, this zoo has elephants, tigers, cheetah, deer and one of the largest gorilla colonies in the world.

Richborough Castle (22-23)

The Romans landed here in AD 43 and called their settlement 'Rutupiae'; a monument was erected in AD 85 but only rubble survives. In the 3rd century, it was fortified with a triple line of ditches but was soon replaced by a Saxon Shore Fort, one of a series built to protect the coast. Three massive sets of walls remain. A little way south is the 'Gallows Field', the town's execution site.

Bekesbourne   Littlebourne   Wickhambreaux   Grove Hill   Preston   Elmstone   Upper Goldstone

1 From the Tourist Information Centre L, then sharp R onto Delf Street past Fleur de Lys PH. SA on King Street. At T-j by Millwall Place R, then L 'Station'

2 After 1 mile at roundabout L, 'A258 Deal', then 2nd R on Mill Lane 'Ham'

3 After ¾ mile 1st L by triangle of grass 'Finglesham, Deal'

➡ **page 100**

18 At X-roads with A257 in Littlebourne SA onto Margate Street 'Ickham, Wickhambreaux'

19 Follow signs for Preston through Wickhambreaux. After 3 miles by triangle of grass R 'Preston 1¼, Wingham 3¾'

20 At T-j with B2046 in Preston R 'Wingham, Canterbury', then L opposite village stores and phone box 'Elmstone ¾, Westmarsh 3'

21 Follow signs for Elmstone then Westmarsh. On RH bend after 1 mile L towards church 'Sheerwater ¾, Hoaden 1¼, Westmarsh 1½'

22 Follow signs for Ware then Richborough. At T-j / X-roads L 'Richborough'

23 At T-j by fire station in Sandwich L to return to town centre

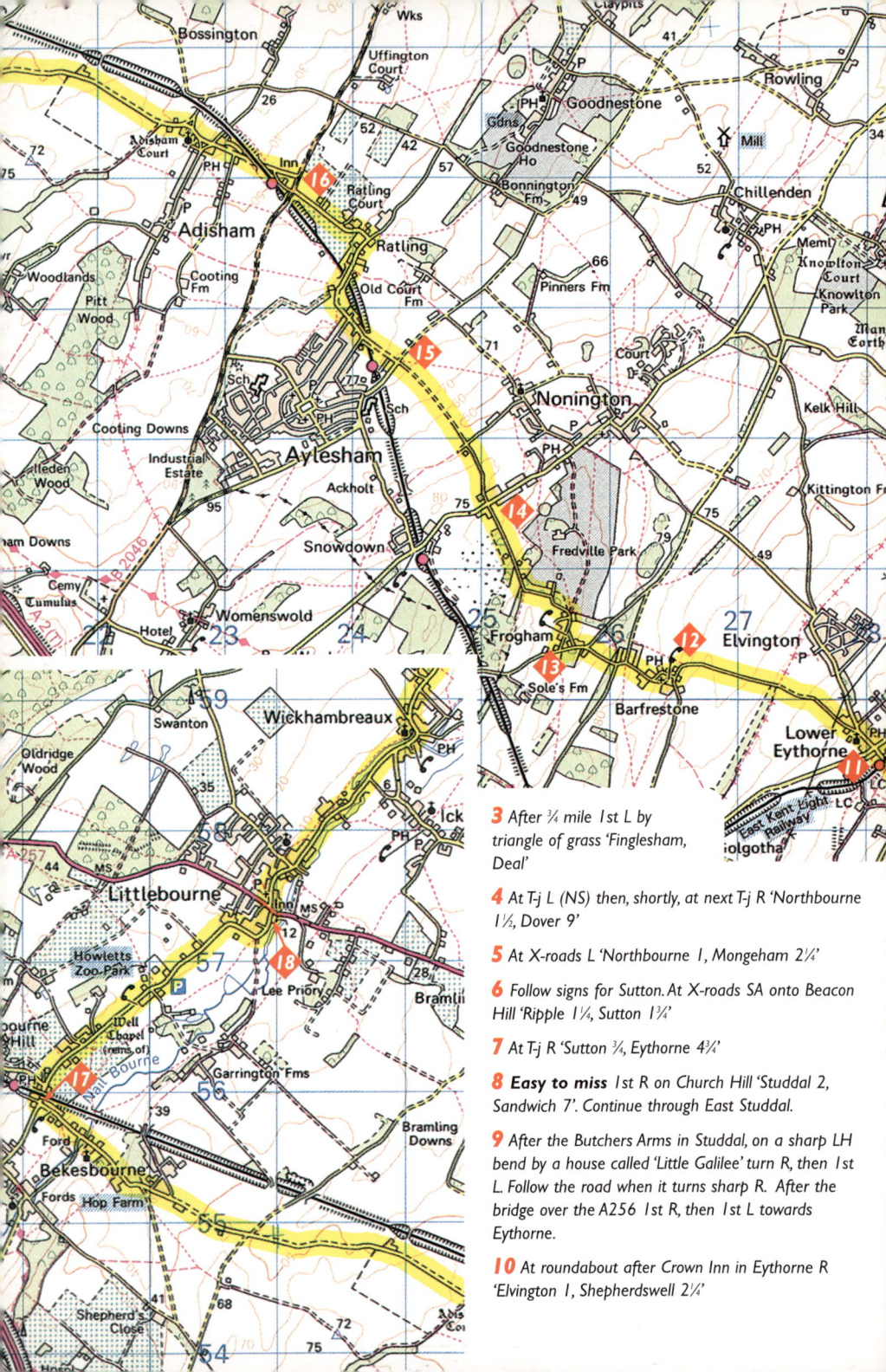

3 After ¾ mile 1st L by triangle of grass 'Finglesham, Deal'

4 At T-j L (NS) then, shortly, at next T-j R 'Northbourne 1½, Dover 9'

5 At X-roads L 'Northbourne 1, Mongeham 2¼'

6 Follow signs for Sutton. At X-roads SA onto Beacon Hill 'Ripple 1¼, Sutton 1¾'

7 At T-j R 'Sutton ¾, Eythorne 4¾'

8 *Easy to miss* 1st R on Church Hill 'Studdal 2, Sandwich 7'. Continue through East Studdal.

9 After the Butchers Arms in Studdal, on a sharp LH bend by a house called 'Little Galilee' turn R, then 1st L. Follow the road when it turns sharp R. After the bridge over the A256 1st R, then 1st L towards Eythorne.

10 At roundabout after Crown Inn in Eythorne R 'Elvington 1, Shepherdswell 2¼'

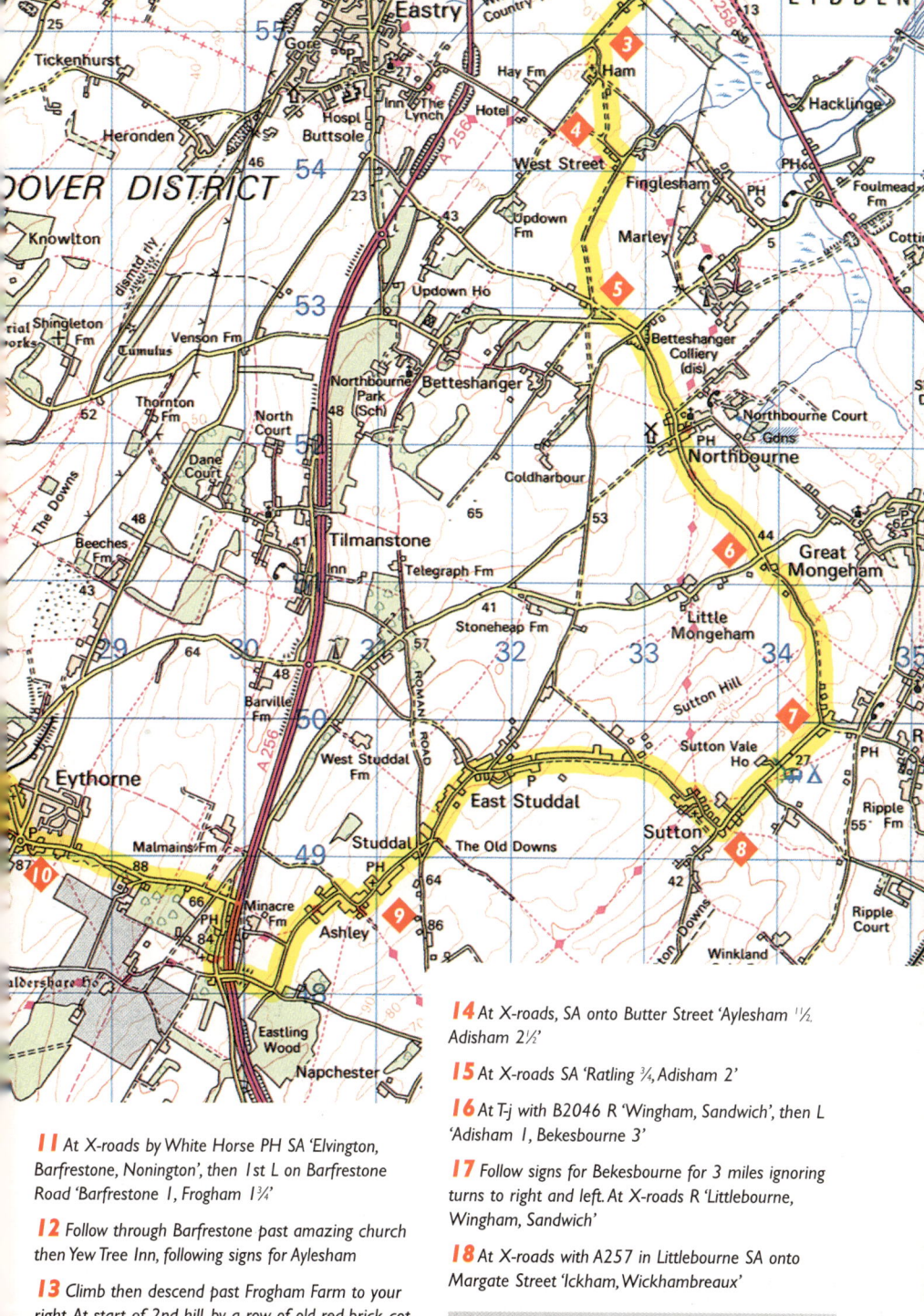

11 At X-roads by White Horse PH SA 'Elvington, Barfrestone, Nonington', then 1st L on Barfrestone Road 'Barfrestone 1, Frogham 1¾'

12 Follow through Barfrestone past amazing church then Yew Tree Inn, following signs for Aylesham

13 Climb then descend past Frogham Farm to your right. At start of 2nd hill, by a row of old red-brick cottages R 'Nonington 1, Aylesham 1¾'

14 At X-roads, SA onto Butter Street 'Aylesham 1½, Adisham 2½'

15 At X-roads SA 'Ratling ¾, Adisham 2'

16 At T-j with B2046 R 'Wingham, Sandwich', then L 'Adisham 1, Bekesbourne 3'

17 Follow signs for Bekesbourne for 3 miles ignoring turns to right and left. At X-roads R 'Littlebourne, Wingham, Sandwich'

18 At X-roads with A257 in Littlebourne SA onto Margate Street 'Ickham, Wickhambreaux'

◀ **page 99**

Along the Greensand Way south of Godalming

Try this ride just to prove that you do not need to drive down to the South Downs to use your mountain bike! There is a plethora of bridleways in the triangle formed by Godalming, Haslemere and Billingshurst, and this route simply links up a few of them. Why not make up a route of your own by linking up a few others? This is a ride for old footwear and long trousers, which, despite these minor drawbacks, contains some fine views, good climbs and a few surprises.

Start

White Horse PH, Hascombe

 P Car park 1 mile north of the start at Winkworth Arboretum

Distance and grade

15 miles

 Easy/moderate

Terrain

No major climbs, though some hills may be tough after rain or in winter because of mud. If you manage the first hill, you will manage the rest!

Nearest railway

Milford, 1 mile from the route at Enton

Refreshments

*White Horse PH ●●, **Hascombe***
*Kings Arms PH ●, lots of choice in **Godalming***
*Merry Harriers PH ●, **North of Hambledon***

Hascombe

Nore

Scotsland Farm

Selhurst Common

Nurscombe Farm

Busbridge

Places of interest

Bramley (8)

This village has some attractive buildings including two Lutyens houses, the 16th-century Bramley East Manor in the High Street and some fine Regency and Georgian houses. A 13th-century chancel and the remains of a Norman arch can be seen in Holy Trinity Church.

Hambledon (23)

School Cottage, Malthouse Cottage and Malthouse Farm are good examples of 16th- and 17th-century cottages; parts of the church are much older (14th-century) and Court Farm and the Granary are also interesting. The surrounding hills give good views over the downs.

Woodland track near Hyde stile

Great Enton

Enton Hall

Burgate House

1 Facing the White Horse PH, take track to right of it 'Private Road, Hascombe Place Farm'. Continue in same direction beyond farm uphill on bridleway

2 You will soon come to the muddiest section of the ride. The first 100 yards are the worst and there are two more bad stretches in this climb

3 Up and over hill. At T-j by green gate L.

4 After 1 mile, at T-j with road R, then 1st L after ½ mile on Gate Street. Continue to the end of the tarmac, past farm 'No exit, Keepers only'. Follow in same direction as it becomes single track. (May be muddy, be prepared for nettles)

5 In woodland, by signpost with yellow arrow indicating footpath to the left R, then L following blue arrows

6 Briefly join gravel drive. After 100 yards, on RH bend L (in effect SA) uphill on earth track

7 This track joins more major track near house (Bramley Park). Just past house at T-j of tracks L, following wooden fence around

8 At times muddy (nettles). Follow track around Eastwater Barn to tarmac drive by pond. At road L

9 After 1 mile, shortly after fine parkland of Thornecombe House on your left R on tarmac drive opposite metal railings 'Public Bridleway'

10 Tarmac turns to track and climbs steeply then more gently. At X-roads of bridleways near top of hill by 4-way signpost SA. At road L past large red-brick tower

11 At T-j with B2130 SA just to the left of Busbridge Parish Council Noticeboard onto dead-end road

12 At T-j at the end of North Munstead Lane R, then at next T-j at the end of Hambledon Road L 'Milford, Eashing'

13 Shortly after passing nursing home on left, opposite Busbridge Lane on right L onto public bridleway

14 Descend to pass between lakes. Climb steeply. At road at the end of the drive to Clock Barn Farm SA 'Public Bridleway, Inwood Cottage'

15 Just before house and 'Private' sign L on track into woodland

16 At road by sign for nurseries R

17 **Easy to miss.** At next T-j SA onto track 'National Trust, Hydon's Ball', then immediately leave main track and turn R onto narrower bridleway

18 Track widens. At X-roads of bridleways SA. At road then L 'Public Bridleway, Potters Hill'

19 Through farm, across two fairways of the golf course (watch out for golf balls!) in the same direction. At road R

20 Shortly after Enton Hall on left L by pond 'Public bridleway'

21 **Easy to miss.** Follow broad gravel track gently uphill for ½ mile passing white gate of Sweetwater Cottage on the right. Just past signpost for Busses Cottage on the right fork L (blue arrow)

22 At times muddy. At road by the Merry Harriers PH R, then after 400 yards 1st L onto Church Lane 'Hambledon Church'

23 Bear R by church through parking area 'Public bridleway'

24 At T-j with broader track R (red arrow), then immediately L steeply uphill onto narrow sunken track. After 200 yards take LH, higher fork (ignore signpost pointing down to the right). This section may be overgrown

25 Follow through woodland then RH edge of field (good views to right). Descend through woodland to road

26 At road R, then L 'Public bridleway'. Follow main track over X-roads of tracks

27 Follow broad gravel track down to small road and turn R. At T-j with B2130 R to return to White Horse PH

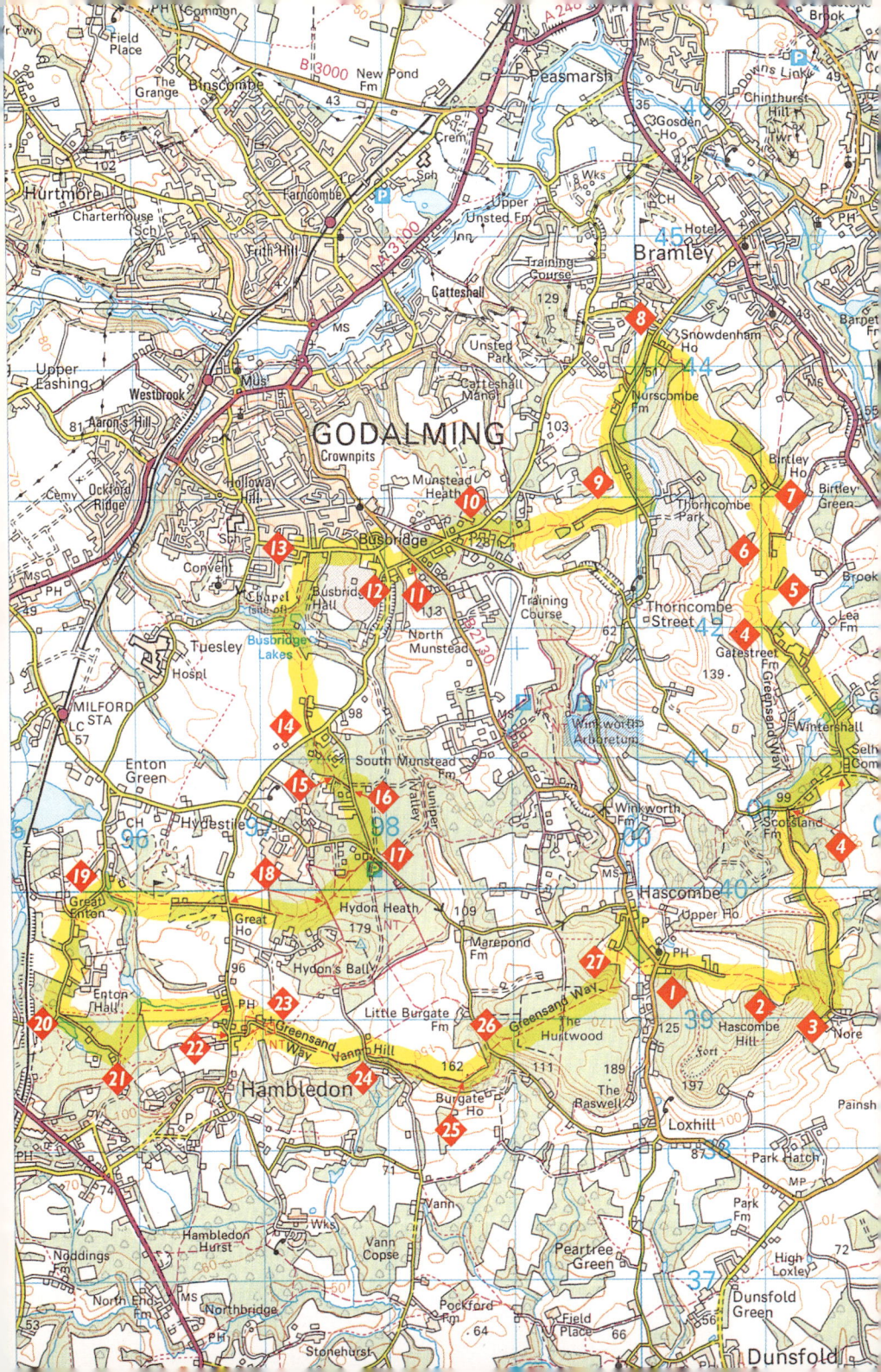

Glorious downland riding near Goodwood

The ride takes in some of the very best scenery at the western end of the South Downs. Each of the five climbs is rewarded with either great views, a great descent or both. There is a satisfying mixture of woodland and open downland and the opportunity to stop at one or two of the excellent pubs on the way. You may even get a chance to race against the horses at Goodwood if you turn up on a race day!

Start

The car park 2 miles south of Singleton off the A286 on the west side of St Roche's Hill

P As above

Distance and grade

23 miles

Moderate/strenuous

Terrain

Five climbs of between 400 and 450 feet, some pushing required; downs and woodland

Nearest railway

Fishbourne, 4 miles south of the route at Kingley Vale Nature Reserve or Petersfield, 6 miles west of North Marden

1 *From car park cross road onto track. At fork by ruined house bear L away from the woodland on the right and along the field edge on fine gentle descent*

2 *Through gate into open field. Bear slightly L downhill. Through gate in same direction towards road and houses*

3 *At T-j with A286 R, then L 'Binderton Lane'*

4 *At B2141 R, then L on bridleway*

 page 109

20 *At A286 SA onto track 'South Downs Way'*

21 **Easy to miss.** *Climb to top of hill, go past hut on stilts and trig point on your left and through X-roads of footpaths. ¼ mile past the brow of the hill at 4-way signpost turn R onto grassy track at right angles to South Downs Way downhill into wood.*

22 *At X-roads with forestry track SA. At T-j with next forestry track R 'Public Bridleway'*

23 *Follow major track to X-roads. Turn L 'Petworth 10, East Dean 1'*

24 *Just past Fox PH R towards telephone box, then L at triangle of grass*

25 *Climb steadily for a mile on major track past racecourse to road. At road R*

26 *Follow racecourse on right. At T-j R 'Singleton 2, Midhurst 8', then L opposite grandstand '6 Label Only'*

27 *Follow track to the left of iron railings. At gate SA into open field, contouring to join better defined track and to return to start*

Binderton House   Stoke Down   Stoughton   Locksash Farm   Telegraph Hill   North Marden   Hooksway

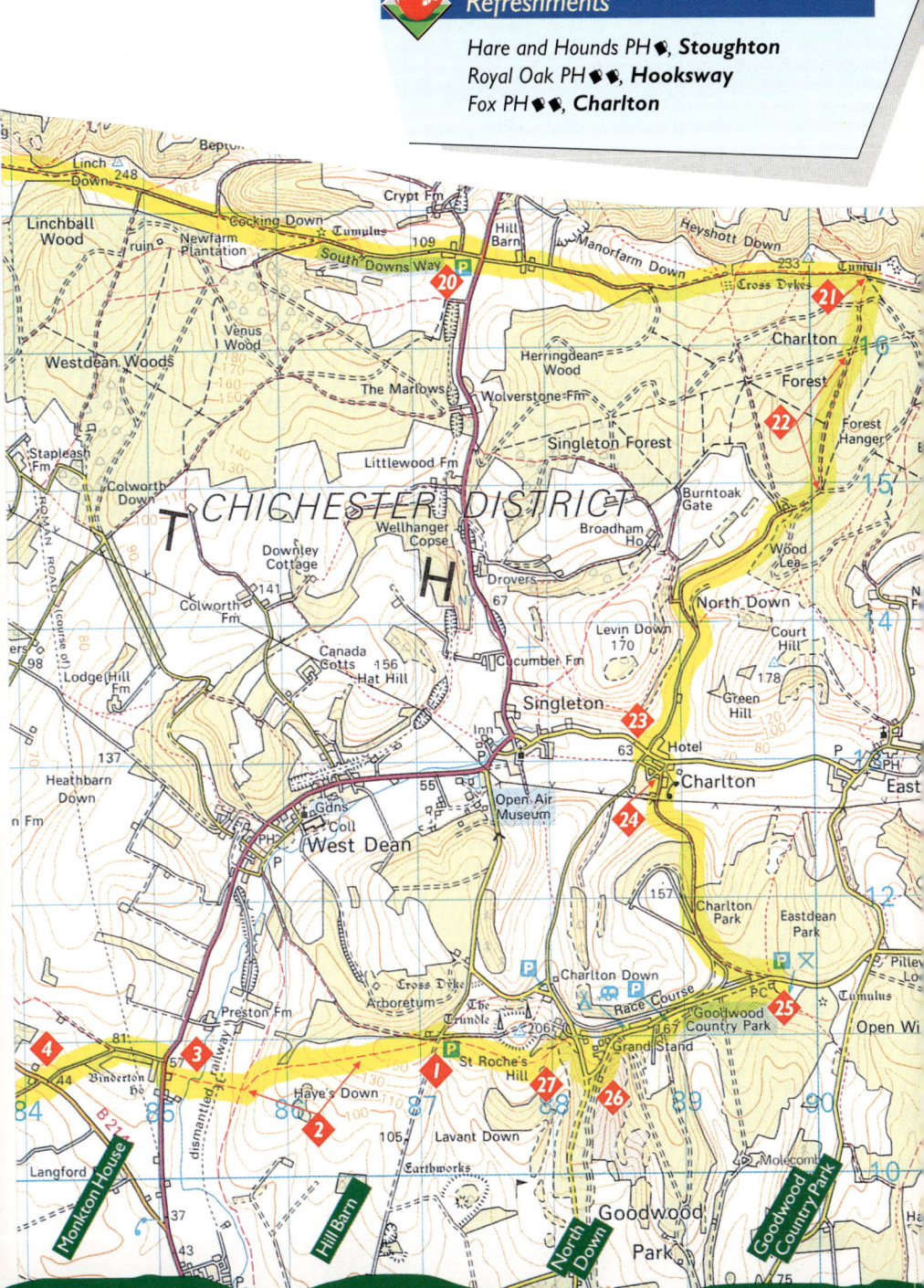

107

Places of interest

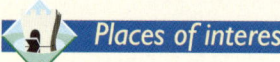

West Dean Gardens (3)

These informal gardens are slightly off the route. Within the 30 acres are a gazebo, a pergola, some outstanding trees, a spring garden, a wild garden and a walled garden.

The Mardens (14-18)

North (17), East (nr.18), Up (nr.15) and West (nr.14) Marden are connected by lanes twisting between the fields and woods; a very peaceful area.

Compton (15)

Lying in a wooded valley a little off the route, Compton consists of a few attractive cottages, a church, a pub and a shop.

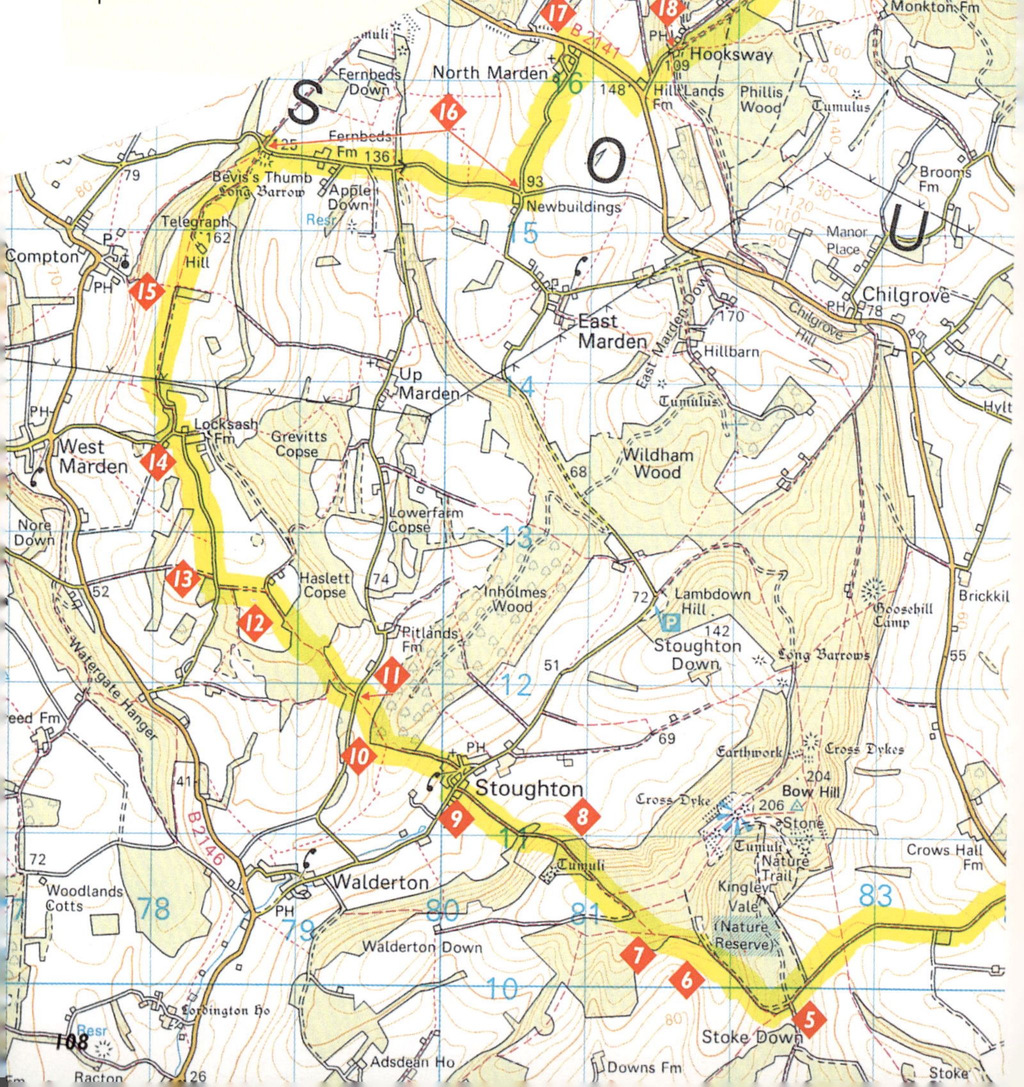

5 Follow this track for 1¼ miles over X-roads of bridleways. At sign for Kingley Vale follow the wood on your right closely, turning R uphill to follow wood edge 'Nature Conservancy. National Nature Reserve. Kingley Vale'

6 At fork in clearing L along edge of fence

7 At fork in very gloomy stretch of woodland R on the steeper uphill track. At next fork R uphill with wood close to the right

8 After brow of hill, by breeze block base take main track into wood for superb descent

9 At road R, then 1st L towards telephone box. At fork bear L 'Public Bridleway'

10 Steep climb. Fork L along edge of wood. Descend to road

11 At road SA. At fork after 200 yards R very steeply uphill

12 Follow main track until reaching sharp bend in major well-made track with sign for 'Lye Common, No Riding' to your right. Turn L.

13 At road R

14 After ¾ mile, shortly after sharp LH bend in road by a large square house R onto track by double metal gate

15 Follow main track with wood on right. This track becomes narrow with hedgerow on left. Follow towards house and trees on top of Telegraph Hill and take main track to road

16 At T-j with road R following signs for North Marden. At T-j L 'North Marden'

17 At T-j with B2141 R 'Chichester 8½'. At top of hill L 'Royal Oak PH', 'Hooksway ¼'

18 Once past PH take middle of three tracks

19 Join the South Downs Way. Climb out of woods, past trig point then a fast descent to the road

 **page 107**

Goodwood House

West from Amberley on the South Downs Way over Bignor Hill to East Dean

Start

Railway station at Amberley

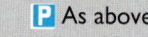 As above

Distance and grade

19 miles

Moderate/strenuous

Terrain

A long, at times steep, climb of 750 feet from Amberley to the masts beyond Bignor Hill, a climb of 280 feet from the A285 to the X-roads with the South Downs Way, and one of 380 feet from Droke Forestry Car Park to just below the masts

Nearest railway

Amberley

A kill-or-cure climb at the start of this ride takes you from sea level at the tidal River Arun near Amberley up over Bignor Hill, with the views opening up behind you with each revolution of the pedals (any excuse for a stop!). The route leaves the South Downs Way near the car park on Bignor Hill because the climb on the other side of the A285 is through a ploughed field. Broaden your horizons – there are numerous bridlepaths to be explored either side of the South Downs Way. Once you have arrived at Tegleaze, to the west of the A285, prepare for a magnificent descent into East Dean. There is a chance to refuel before you climb through the woods and follow the ridge west back to the roundabout by the A284. A very fast road descent should get rid of most of the mud on your bike!

Refreshments

Bridge Inn ☂, Black Horse PH ☂, Boat House PH, Cafe, **Amberley**
Hurdlemakers PH ☂, **East Dean**
George and Dragon PH ☂☂, **Houghton**
Tea stop at **car park near A29 A284 roundabout**

Amberley Station
Houghton
Westburton Hill
Bignor Hill
Barlavington Down
Duncton Down

Places of interest

Arundel (19)

The great Norman castle is quite a long way south of the route but Arundel Park is nearer. There is a large Wildfowl Trust reserve with exotic swans, geese and ducks.

Off-road riding tips

- Padded shorts and gloves make off-road riding more comfortable

- If there is any possibility of rain take something waterproof. Never underestimate the effects of wind-chill when you are wet, even in summer

- In wet and cold conditions keep a layer of warm clothes next to the skin – thermal underwear or wool

- After fixing a puncture, check the inside of the tyre for embedded thorns before replacing the inner tube. A screwdriver is useful for winkling out difficult thorns

- If your brake blocks look as though they are wearing thin, take a spare set with you. New brake blocks are much cheaper than new rims

- Take a compass with you for crossing moorland or in poor visibility and know how to use it

East Dean   Droke   Selhurst Park   Whiteways Lodge   Houghton

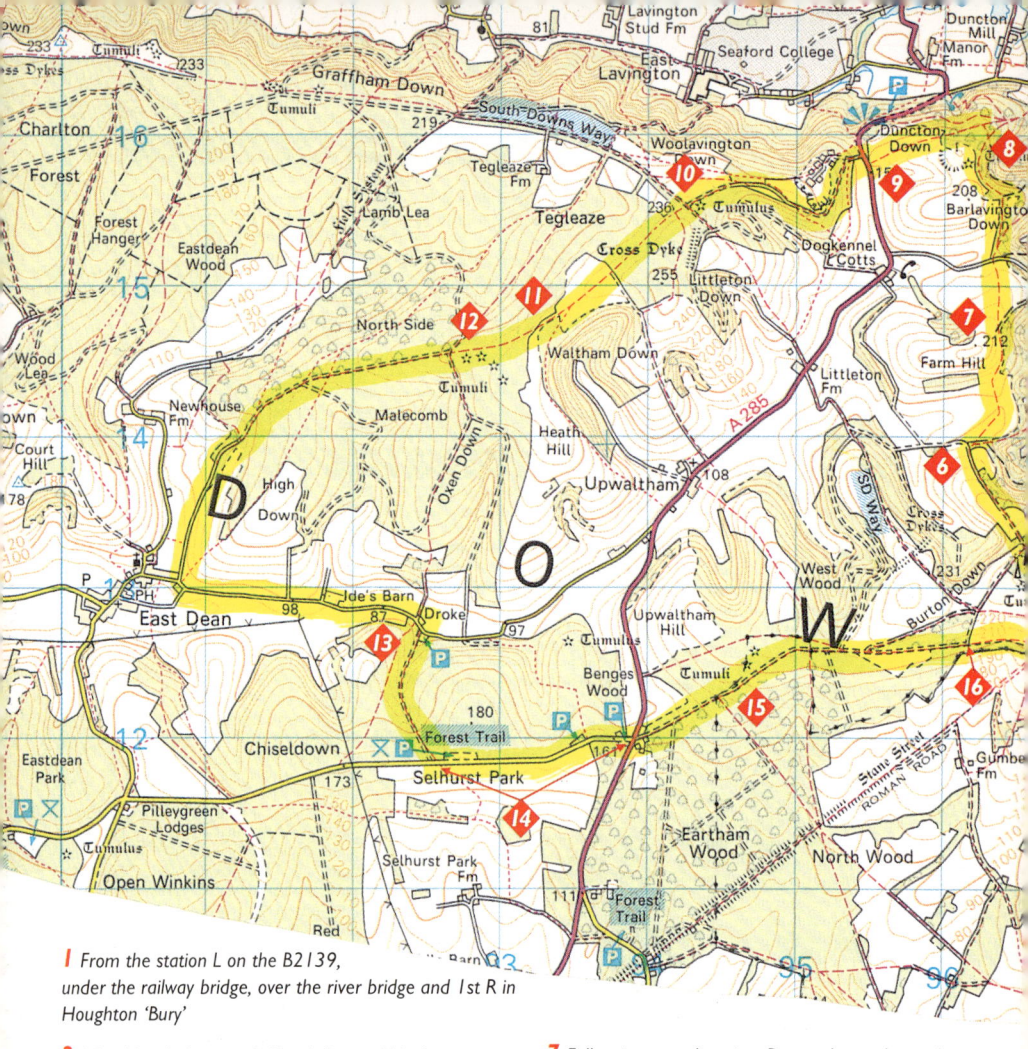

1 *From the station L on the B2139, under the railway bridge, over the river bridge and 1st R in Houghton 'Bury'*

2 *After ¼ mile L on track 'South Downs Way'*

3 *Steep climb. At T-j with A29 R, then L on continuation of South Downs Way*

4 *Follow South Downs Way, just past barn, dog-leg L then R, steeply uphill over Bignor Hill to car park/end of tarmac road/sign with Latin names*

5 *Through car park, following South Downs Way signs through wooden barrier ('No cars'). After 100 yards, leave South Downs Way and bear R uphill on broad stony track ('Public bridleway') towards, then to the right of masts*

6 Easy to miss. *Go past patch of woodland to the right then a field. Just **before** start of second patch of woodland, leave the main track and turn R 'Public Bridleway' following the wire fence on the right. Shortly, at 3-way split take LH track*

7 *Follow in same direction. Descend to go beneath power lines carried by telegraph poles then climb towards wood on hill (maybe overgrown)*

8 *On the descent in the wood at a fork by a signpost L 'Public bridleway', then shortly, at T-j with more major track (3-way signpost) L uphill*

9 *Exit wood, cross field. At road R then L 'Duncton Quarrying'. Just before gate to quarry L uphill on broad chalk path*

10 *At X-roads with South Downs Way by a large wooden post with 'Tegleaze' written on it SA 'East Dean'*

11 *Cross clearing on grassy track. Through gate onto stony track. 100 yards after rejoining woodland on right, just before the main track ends at a gate into a field R on smaller track into forest*

12 At major X-roads of forestry tracks SA downhill on long straight track

13 At road L (or R for PH/stores). After a mile, at a car park by Forestry Commission sign for 'Droke Forest' R uphill on gravel track into wood

14 At road L. At T-j with A285 by St Mary's Farm SA 'Public bridleway'

15 Woodland climb, then through clearing and along RH edge of woodland with fine views to right

16 At major fork of tracks at the edge of the woodland you have been following on your left, with the masts diagonally uphill to your left, SA 'Public Bridleway' along the LH edge of woodland

17 At X-roads of bridleways, with a large field to your right, SA into woodland 'Public Bridleway'. At junction with more major track SA 'Public Bridleway'

18 At next X-roads, near a wooden bench and a National Trust sign for Bignor Hill SA with field to left and wood to right. Good descent through woodland then clearing, bearing L at the bottom of the clearing

19 At major forestry X-roads SA to arrive at Whiteways Picnic Site. At roundabout L on B2139 'Amberley, Storrington' for a fast road descent to return to Amberley

4 East from Amberley over Wepham Down and Rackham Hill

There is a lot of breezy, open downland on this ride and the fine views one expects (and deserves) from the top of the ridges. The ride starts with a steep road climb, followed by a descent into and climb out of a steep valley (can you do it without getting off?). The route continues down into the quiet tucked-away village of Burpham, which has a fine pub. A woodland stretch follows, leaving the trees just as the going starts to get muddy. The section above Lower Barpham is wonderful, perched right on the edge of the very steep hillside. As you continue to climb, views open up on both sides before the descent to Lee Farm. A final climb onto Rackham Hill gives views over the Arun Valley and sets you up for the last descent.

Start

Railway station at Amberley

P As above

Distance and grade

15 miles

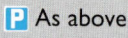

Moderate/strenuous

Terrain

Three major climbs: 330 feet from Amberley to Downs Farm, 470 feet from Burpham to Barpham Hill and 360 feet from Lee Farm to Rackham Hill

Nearest railway

Amberley

Refreshments

Bridge Inn ♦, Black Horse PH ♦, Boat House PH, cafe, **Amberley** George and Dragon PH ♦♦, **Burpham**

Amberley Station

Downs Farm

The Burgh

Peppering High Barn

Burpham

Wepham Wood

Places of interest

Burpham (6)

A hamlet with brick and flint thatched cottages and a Norman church overlooking the water-meadows.

Off-road riding tips

- Lower your saddle when going down steep off-road sections, keep the pedals level, stand up out of the saddle to let your legs absorb the bumps and keep your weight over the rear wheel

- If using a jet spray to clean your bike, do not aim the hose directly at the hubs or bottom bracket but clean these parts from above

- Lubricate your bike after washing it or after a very wet ride, paying particular attention to the chain

- Carry a water bottle in the bottle carrier and keep it filled, particularly on hot days

- Good energy foods which don't take up much space are dates, figs, dried fruit and nuts

- Good equipment doesn't make you a good cyclist. The only bad cyclists are those who show no consideration to others, whether by weaving around, failing to indicate or riding on pavements in on-road situations, or by failing to follow the countryside code, and showing no respect to walkers and horseriders when off-road

- Always take a few coins for emergencies

- Make sure there is nothing loose and dangling (laces, daypack straps, pannier straps) which may get caught in the spokes, chain or pedals

Barpham Hill   Wepham Down   Lee Farm   Springhead Hill   Rackham Hill   Amberley Mount   Downs Farm

1 Out of car park R, then after ½ mile 1st R on High Titten. Climb on tarmac towards round storage bins

2 Just before large round storage bins L on track 'No vehicles except access'. Continue past farm buildings. At fork take RH, lower track (**not** South Downs Way), then after 100 yards R at next fork

3 On descent, at fork bear R to stay close to the fence on your right. Descend into the valley and climb steeply

4 Through gate. At T-j of tracks at top of hill by a 4-way signpost R then 100 yards before farm buildings L sharply back on yourself

5 On broad track past farm and onto tarmac. 1st R by triangle of grass (NS), then 1st L opposite Peppering Farm passing The Garden House on your right

6 Past George and Dragon PH, then on sharp LH bend 1st R

7 At T-j in Wepham R, then L on concrete track 'Public bridleway'

8 Climb steeply on concrete track. At top of hill on sharp LH bend bear R (in effect SA) 'Public bridleway'

9 At T-j of tracks at the bottom by sign for Angmering Park Estate R, then at fork L. At X-roads by tarmac road L towards farm buildings (this detour avoids a very steep, muddy climb)

10 Ignore 1st bridleway to the left by gate and Angmering Park Estate sign. At X-roads of tracks bear slightly L on broad forestry track (ignore the footpath signposted to the right). After ¾ mile bear R, staying on main track

11 At X-roads with tarmac by red-brick Keepers Cottage SA. After ¾ mile, at fork of tracks L, following fence round

12 May be muddy. At green gate L onto track with fabulous views to the right

13 Emerge out of wood via red gate. SA main stony track. Continue uphill in same direction through double wooden gates and take the RH fork

14 Through field with fine views left and right, towards and through next set of double wooden gates. Grassy descent. At T-j with broad track R

15 Past farm. At barn at bottom of hill, on RH bend L uphill through double metal gates

16 Climb steadily for 1¼ miles (350 feet climb). At T-j at the top L. Follow signs for South Downs Way for 3½ miles back into Amberley

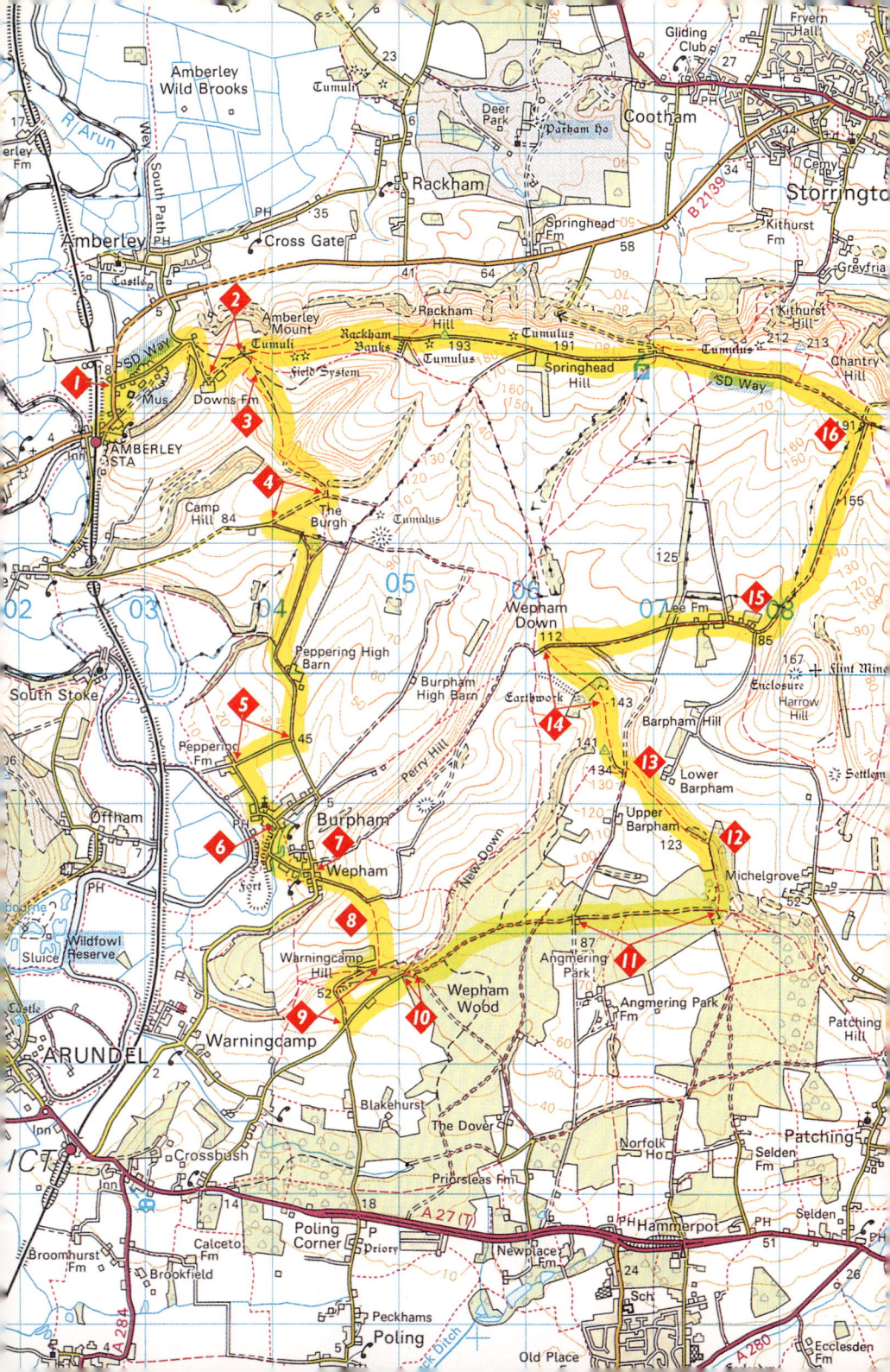

North of Worthing: Cissbury Ring to the Adur Valley and Chanctonbury

Findon is one of those small but perfectly formed villages for cyclists: two pubs, a tea shop, a shop open seven days a week, even a bike shop! The route climbs towards Cissbury Ring, a massive Iron Age hill fort on the site of Neolithic flint mines. This route passes below Cissbury Ring, but if you do visit it, please follow the waymarks and do not stray from the bridleways. The route continues over downland towards the impressive architecture of Lancing College. A road section along the Adur Valley provides resting time before the major climb via the South Downs Way to Chanctonbury Ring. Sadly, this magnificent copse of beech trees was savaged by the great gale of 1987, but the views remain spectacular.

Start

Car park by village green, Findon

P Near village green or on Stable Lane, Findon or in car park beneath Cissbury Ring if there is no space in Findon (join route at instruction 4)

Distance and grade

16 miles

Moderate/strenuous

Terrain

Two climbs: 250 feet from Findon to Cissbury Ring and almost 800 feet from the Adur Valley to Chanctonbury Ring

Nearest railway

Lancing, 1½ miles from the route at its southeast corner

Refreshments

Village House Hotel, Gun Inn 🍴, Green Welly cafe and tea shop, **Findon**

Findon Cissbury Ring Canada Bottom Steep Down

Places of interest

St Mary's, Bramber (11)

This well-preserved timbered house was built in around 1470 and has some fine panelled rooms. The 'Painted Room' is particularly well-known and was decorated for a visit of Elizabeth I.

Steyning (12-13)

This small town is slightly off the route but has some interesting old buildings including a Norman church with nave and chancel arch, a tiled Market House with a clock turret, a medieval poor-house and some 15th-century houses along the High Street.

Chanctonbury Ring (13)

There are excellent views over the countryside from these prehistoric earthworks. The fort is well-known for the trees planted within its walls.

Off-road riding tips

● Keep some spare dry clothes and shoes in the car to change into and carry some bin liners in the car to put dirty, wet clothes in

● Keep other possessions dry in very wet weather by carrying them in two sets of plastic bags

● Experiment with saddle height, forwards and backwards adjustment of saddle, tilt of saddle up or down and height of the handlebars (do not exceed maximum height) until you find your most comfortable riding position

● Anticipate hills by changing into the right gear before it gets tough

● If there is an easier gear when struggling up a hill use it, and let the bike do the work not your knee joints

● Alter your starting point to take account of the wind direction so that you are not cycling back into the wind when you are tired

● If there is any possibilty of cycling in twilight or darkness, take lights with you. As a precaution in winter, take a reflective belt

Bottolphs

Steyning
Round Hill

Chanctonbury
Ring

Gallops Farm

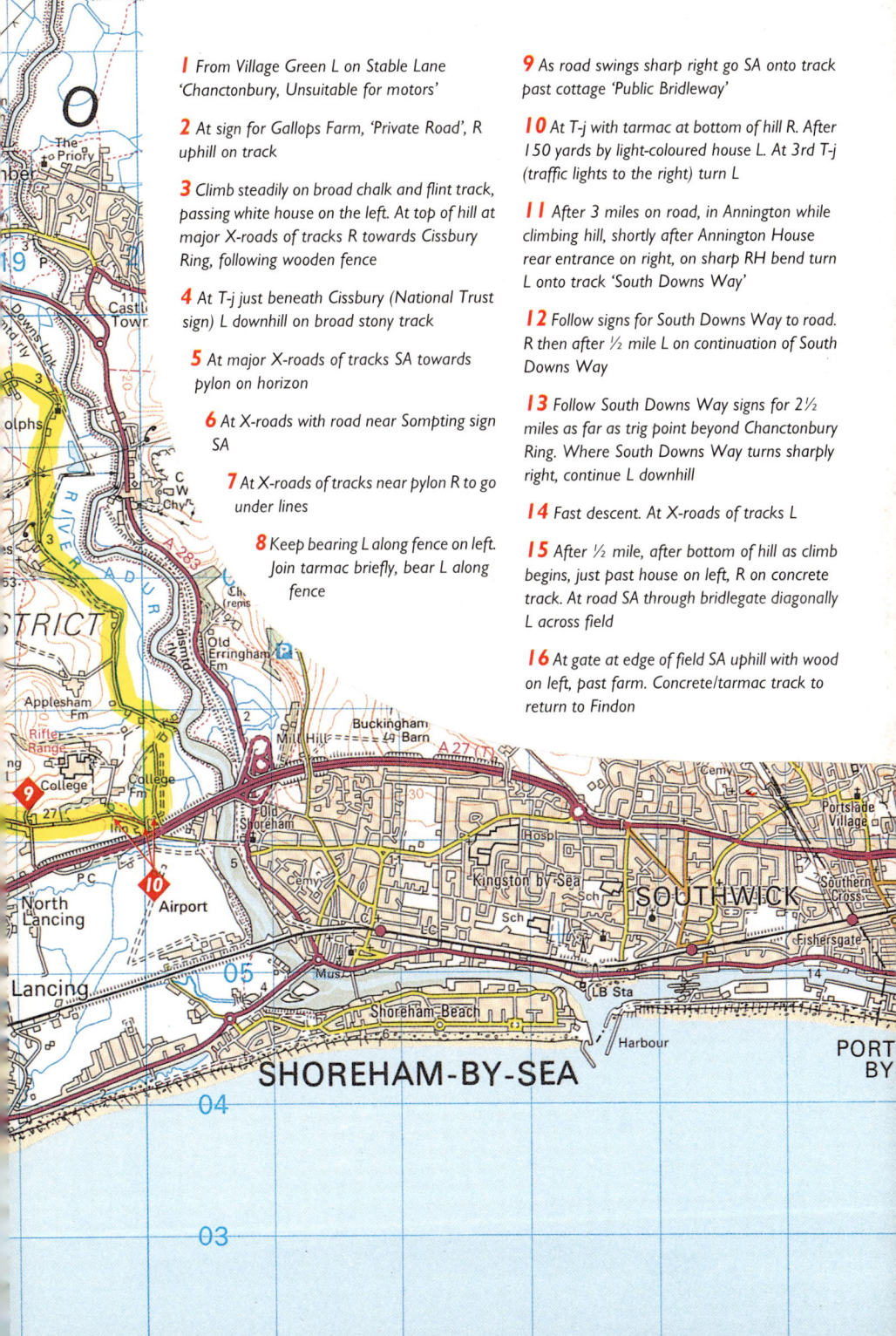

1 From Village Green L on Stable Lane 'Chanctonbury, Unsuitable for motors'

2 At sign for Gallops Farm, 'Private Road', R uphill on track

3 Climb steadily on broad chalk and flint track, passing white house on the left. At top of hill at major X-roads of tracks R towards Cissbury Ring, following wooden fence

4 At T-j just beneath Cissbury (National Trust sign) L downhill on broad stony track

5 At major X-roads of tracks SA towards pylon on horizon

6 At X-roads with road near Sompting sign SA

7 At X-roads of tracks near pylon R to go under lines

8 Keep bearing L along fence on left. Join tarmac briefly, bear L along fence

9 As road swings sharp right go SA onto track past cottage 'Public Bridleway'

10 At T-j with tarmac at bottom of hill R. After 150 yards by light-coloured house L. At 3rd T-j (traffic lights to the right) turn L

11 After 3 miles on road, in Annington while climbing hill, shortly after Annington House rear entrance on right, on sharp RH bend turn L onto track 'South Downs Way'

12 Follow signs for South Downs Way to road. R then after ½ mile L on continuation of South Downs Way

13 Follow South Downs Way signs for 2½ miles as far as trig point beyond Chanctonbury Ring. Where South Downs Way turns sharply right, continue L downhill

14 Fast descent. At X-roads of tracks L

15 After ½ mile, after bottom of hill as climb begins, just past house on left, R on concrete track. At road SA through bridlegate diagonally L across field

16 At gate at edge of field SA uphill with wood on left, past farm. Concrete/tarmac track to return to Findon

West from Alfriston over the Downs to Firle Beacon

Alfriston is a honey pot for tourists arriving by the coachload; but have no fear: this ride escapes quickly onto the Downs where the coaches cannot go. A long steady climb on the South Downs Way brings you to the ridge with magnificent views back across the Cuckmere Valley and down across the Sussex Weald. At times it is hard to believe that you are in the densely populated southeast of England with such big open spaces and views all around. A fast descent via Norton and Bishopstone, with a little negotiation of a housing development, brings you to the start of the second climb. Dodge those golf balls as you make your way across the golf course back onto the ridge for the final swoop into Alfriston.

Refreshments

Star PH ♦♦, lots of choice in **Alfriston**
Ram PH ♦♦, **West Firle** (almost 500 feet height loss)

Start

The square, Alfriston

P Long-term car park in Alfriston (turn up early) or turn R opposite George Inn and park in 'Kings Ride leading to Broadway' or some parking on the track at the top end of the village (instruction 2)

Distance and grade

13 miles

Moderate/strenuous

Terrain

Two climbs: 650 feet from Alfriston to Firle Beacon, 530 feet from Norton and Bishopstone back onto the South Downs Way

Nearest railway

Newhaven or Bishopstone, both 1½ miles from the southeast corner of the route, or Berwick, 3 miles north of Alfriston

Alfriston

Long Burgh

Bostal Hill

Firle Beacon

Blackcap Farm

Blackcap Hill

Gardener's Hill

Alfriston (1)

Timbered houses with overhanging storeys line the main street. The large church dominating the green was built out of flint in the shape of a Greek Cross.

Next to the church is the half-timbered Clergy House which was the first building ever to be acquired by the National Trust. It was built for a community of parish priests in 1350 and contains large dining and recreation areas and some smaller rooms; it now houses an exhibition on 'Wealden House Building'. The ancient and interesting Market Cross Inn (once a smugglers' haunt), Star Inn and George Inn are worth visiting.

Alfriston Heritage Centre and Blacksmith's Museum (1)

15th-century buildings contain the old forge, a blacksmith's and farrier's museum. The history of Alfriston is displayed in an annexe.

*The South Downs
Way near Alfriston*

Firle Place (4)

Built in the 16th century, this house was extensively altered between 1713 and 1754. The south side gable and the two courtyards of the original plan survived but most of the house was swallowed up by the new one. Upstairs are fine collections of 18th-century French furniture, Sevres porcelain and some important pictures. The long gallery (built in 1713) overlooks the South Downs and contains interesting works of the English School including David Teniers's 'The Wine Harvest'.

Poverty Bottom

Norton

Bishopstone

Long Burgh

1 From the square, facing tea shop and antiques shop L

2 After ¾ mile at the top of steady climb at X-roads with Winton Street L on broad track

3 At 3-way fork take middle or LH track uphill. At X-roads at top R on South Downs Way

4 Follow South Downs Way for 3½ miles over Firle Beacon towards masts. At car park just before masts L on tarmac road

5 Through farm. Steep descent. Through bridlegate and continue along valley bottom. Follow track as it swings to the right. Climb for 300 yards then at 4-way signpost turn L

6 At X-roads of tracks at the end of the field on your left L downhill towards houses

7 Track becomes tarmac. Bear R at triangle of grass, pass through Norton, descend then climb. At brow of hill in Bishopstone with a row of flint cottages ahead, turn L onto broad track 'Public Bridleway, East Blatchington'

8 Take RH fork after 200 yards then bear R around RH edge of field alongside stone wall. At T-j with road L

9 After ½ mile, at the start of housing estate, by the first street light and a sign for 'Grand Avenue' R down tarmac path. At road SA on continuation of path to emerge at Pilgrims School.

10 At T-j by school L towards no through road. Just by sign for Seaford Golf Club bear L on bridleway 'Bo Peep 3 miles'

11 Through gate onto golf course. Aim to the R of the green and you will soon discover a track climbing to the L between hedgerows

12 Follow this uphill over X-roads with concrete track. At junction of tracks at clearing at top of hill SA through bridlegate (blue arrow)

13 Down then up, following the track in the same direction towards the white post at the end of the big field (stick close to fence on right)

14 Rejoin South Downs Way, turning R along ridge to return to Alfriston. At X-roads of tracks above Alfriston either SA on South Downs Way or L to return by outward route

East from Alfriston via Friston Forest to Jevington and Windover Hill

Be prepared for the hordes of tourists in Alfriston. You will soon leave them behind as you climb steeply towards the top of Lullington Heath and are rewarded with fine views of the impressive valley between Lullington Heath and Windover Hill. A stretch in Friston Forest takes you as far as a vineyard in Westdean. The views have been good, but better still await you from the top of Willingdon Hill, with the English Channel away to the southeast. Jevington has a pub, but its famous chalk figure, The Long Man, lies on the Downs on the route back towards Alfriston.

Refreshments

*Star PH ● ●, lots of choice in **Alfriston**
Eight Bells PH, **Jevington***

Start

The square, Alfriston

🅿 Long-term car park in Alfriston (turn up early) or turn R opposite George Inn and park on 'Kings Ride leading to Broadway'; or use car parks in or near Exceat and join ride at Westdean

Distance and grade

15 miles

Moderate/strenuous

Terrain

Three climbs: 400 feet from Alfriston to Lullington Heath, 530 feet from Friston to the top of Willingdon Hill, 330 feet from Jevington to Windover Hill

Nearest railway

Berwick Station, 3 miles north of Alfriston

Alfriston   Lullington Court   Lullington Heath   Westdean   Friston Hill   Friston

Drusillas (1)

Slightly off the route to the north, Drusillas is a zoo park with large collections of such animals as llamas, monkeys and penguins. There is also an adventure playground, a tropical butterfly house and a miniature railway.

Lullington and Litlington (4)

These pretty villages have interesting churches: Lullington's is the smallest in England and is really just a chancel left from an older church; Litlington's is very old, dating back to about 1150.

The Living World, Seven Sisters Country Park (7)

This is an exotic natural history exhibition where all the exhibits are alive. The displays change according to the season but include praying mantids, tarantulas, giant silk moths and fresh water aquaria. The Country Park contains some beautiful scenery.

Seven Sisters Sheep Centre (10)

The practicalites of working with sheep throughout the year are demonstrated here and there are exhibitions on the history of Downland sheep. Processes in wool spinning and sheep yoghurt and cheese making are also displayed.

Friston and East Dean (10)

St Mary's Church at Friston used to be a landmark for smugglers. The church in East Dean houses an unusual copy of a Norman font.

Willingdon Hill

Jevington

Windover Hill

1 Facing the tea shop and antiques shop in the square R towards the A27, then 1st R 'Lullington ¾, Litlington 1¼'

2 Follow signs for Litlington. At T-j by large black wooden barn R 'Litlington, Seaford', then 1st L on track just past a letter box on your right 'Jevington 2½ miles'

3 Climb on broad track. At T-j with another major track bear L. At top by stone pillar with plaque for 'Lullington Heath' R 'Charleston Bottom' (directions are on the side of wooden post)

4 Fast descent. At junction of six tracks at the bottom of the valley ignore 1st right along valley floor, take next R steeply uphill on stony track 'Snap Hill'

5 Steep climb. At next junction SA 'Friston, Westdean'

6 At next major junction R on straight, broad, grassy track slightly downhill. After ½ mile fork R off main track 'Westdean' (blue arrow)

7 Through clearing, then back into woodland to join better stone-based forestry track. Follow this main track as it swings L uphill and completes a 180 degree turn

8 Climb then descend on broad stone-based track. As it swings sharp left with a large clearing to the left bear R downhill onto chalk/grass track into woodland. Follow in same direction down then steeply up and along RH field edge towards tower. At T-j with tarmac with flint house ahead L

9 Follow this lane as it swings right and climbs. At T-j with road at exit of Friston Forest turn R

10 Near the brow of the hill, before joining the A259, just by the sign for 'Friston' sharply L 'Old Willingdon Rd'

11 Steady climb, fabulous views. At T-j at top of hill with flint barn ruins ahead turn L. At X-roads with South Downs Way by stone marker SA. Just before car park sharp L almost back on yourself through bridlegate 'Bridleway, Jevington 1¼ miles' (**not** the obvious broad chalk track which is the Weald Way)

12 Long grassy descent and short woodland section into Jevington. At T-j at the end of Willingdon Lane, opposite flint cottages R

13 300 yards after Eight Bells PH on your left, opposite Old Post Office L onto Green Lane 'No Through Road'

14 Ignore Weald Way to the right . Track becomes sunken lane beneath a canopy of trees. At fork R then shortly join South Downs Way and bear R. Fork R in a clearing following South Downs Way signs for 2½ miles. At T-j with road SA

15 At T-j with road at bottom of hill by triangle of grass bear R (in effect SA) 'Alfriston'. Cross river. At next T-j L 'Alfriston ½, Seaford 5'

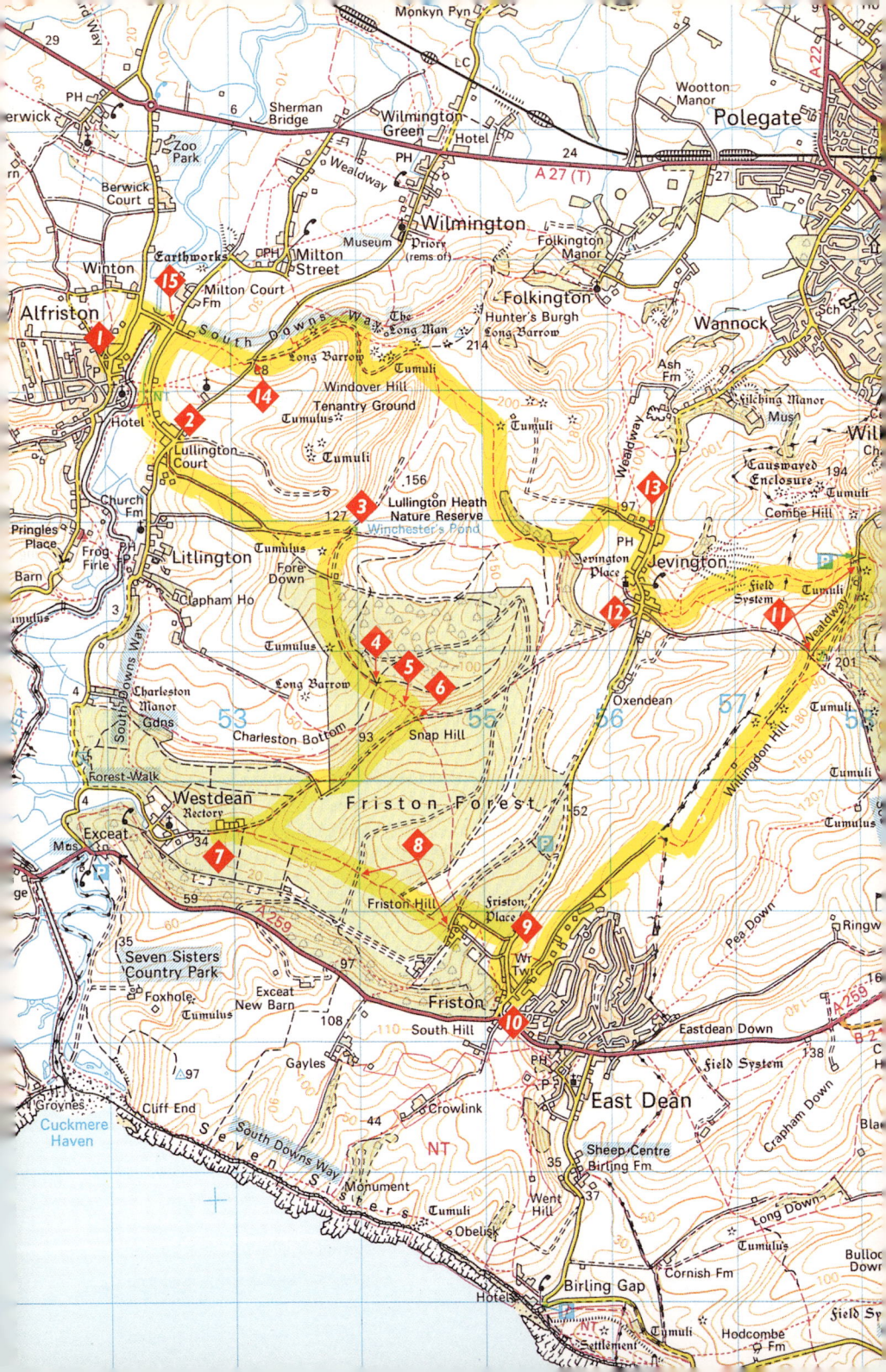

8 From Wye onto the North Downs to northeast of Ashford

The ride wastes no time in getting onto the North Downs Way as it climbs away from the delights of Wye onto the Crundale Downs. There is a particularly lovely section through the woods on a recently improved length of bridleway. If you come across any muddy sections elsewhere on this route write to the local authority (Rights of Way Department), citing the improved stretch as an example of what the paths should be like. A short road section takes you past Sole Street and into Forestry Commission woodland. The smell that may soon have you wrinkling your nostrils comes from a glue factory in the middle of nowhere. Descend to Chilham for a wide range of temptations, then climb again onto the North Downs Way, a joy to follow with its distinctive waymarking.

Start
The church in Wye, 5 miles northeast of Ashford

P Follow signs

Distance and grade
16 miles

Moderate

Terrain
Two 430-foot climbs, one from Wye up onto the Crundale Downs and one from Chilham onto Soakham Downs

Nearest railway
Wye

Wye

Pett Street Farm

Crundale Downs

Sole Street

Places of interest

Withersdane Gardens (1)
Created in the grounds of the Victorian Withersdane Hall, now part of London University, these gardens were designed for teaching purposes. Among the unusual plants found here are pittosporum, trumpet vines and New Zealand flax. The paulownia tree is probably the largest in the country. The herb and pool gardens are best in early summer, the rose garden and main borders are best in mid- to late summer.

Refreshments

New Flying Horse PH *, Tickled Trout PH* *, lots of choice in* **Wye** *Compasses PH* *,* **Sole Street** *Woolpack PH* *, White Horse PH* *, tea shops,* **Chilham**

Godmersham (26)
Slightly off the route and surrounded by parkland, Godmersham is a tiny village. The interesting Palladian house which stands in landscaped gardens overlooking the Stour Valley, was owned by Edward Knight whose sister Jane Austen frequently stayed here. There is a monument to him in the flint church which has a Norman tower and chancel.

Julliberrie Downs   Chilham   Mountain Street   Soakham Downs   Soakham Farm   Boughton Corner

1 With your back to the church, facing the main street L out of town, then 1st L by telephone box on Olantigh Road 'Crundale'

2 After 200 yards, opposite the penultimate red-brick college building R on Occupation Road 'Public Bridleway, North Downs Way'

3 At road SA 'Public bridleway, North Downs Way'

4 Steeply uphill into woodland. At road R

5 At top of hill SA through gate 'Sheep. All dogs on leads', 'No parking'. Follow SA towards wood, through gate and L along edge of wood

6 Follow edge of field gently downhill. Join a wider track. At bottom of decent through woodland, with a gate opening into field ahead R onto track through woodland (blue arrow)

7 At X-roads with concrete track SA

8 At farm buildings, bear L on major track uphill (not marked on map)

9 After a very steep section, as gradient eases just past metal gate sharply L back on yourself (blue arrow)

10 Lovely woodland track, then downland with good views

11 At T-j with road by church R downhill, then steeply uphill

12 At T-j L, then after 400 yards 1st R on track

13 At the end of broad track by a field gate R along edge of woodland (**not** yellow arrow)

14 Along the edge of the wood, then field, then into the next wood on a more major track, following in the same direction on ever-improving surface

15 At T-j with road by Forestry Commission sign 'Denge Wood' L

16 Shortly after passing two brick houses and the glue factory with chimneys on your left, on RH bend go L into wood 'Public Bridleway' on a stone waymark. At fork of tracks at start of wood L on less distinct track

17 At field SA, following line of telegraph poles

18 Through two gates across field in same direction towards wood, crossing beneath telephone wires and through bridlegate

19 At the corner of wood, follow field edge on faint track along LH edge of wood. At the corner of the field follow track into wood, following blue arrows. Take the major track down to tarmac and turn L

20 At T-j with road on sharp bend, L on track 'Byway, Stour Valley Walk'

21 **Easy to miss.** Follow this track for 1½ miles ignoring turnings. At X-roads of tracks by wooden post with blue and yellow arrows and logo for Stour Valley Walk, with double wooden gates 20 yards to your left and a less well-defined, grassier track ahead, follow main track R downhill

22 At main road (A28) R, then 1st L opposite lay-by. At T-j at the end of Branch Road L

23 In square, with entrance to castle ahead L, then at T-j R (in effect SA) 'No Through Road'

24 After a mile, as road bears left to Hurst Farm SA onto woodland track 'No cars, motorbikes except access', 'North Downs Way'

25 Follow main track as it turns R uphill, then L near top of hill, following signs for 'North Downs Way'

26 From here onwards for 2½ miles follow the red arrows indicating the North Downs Way as far as Soakham Farm, then the road

27 At road L. At offset X-roads with A28 SA 'Wye, Brook, Hastingleigh'

28 After railway crossing 1st L 'Car Park' to return to church

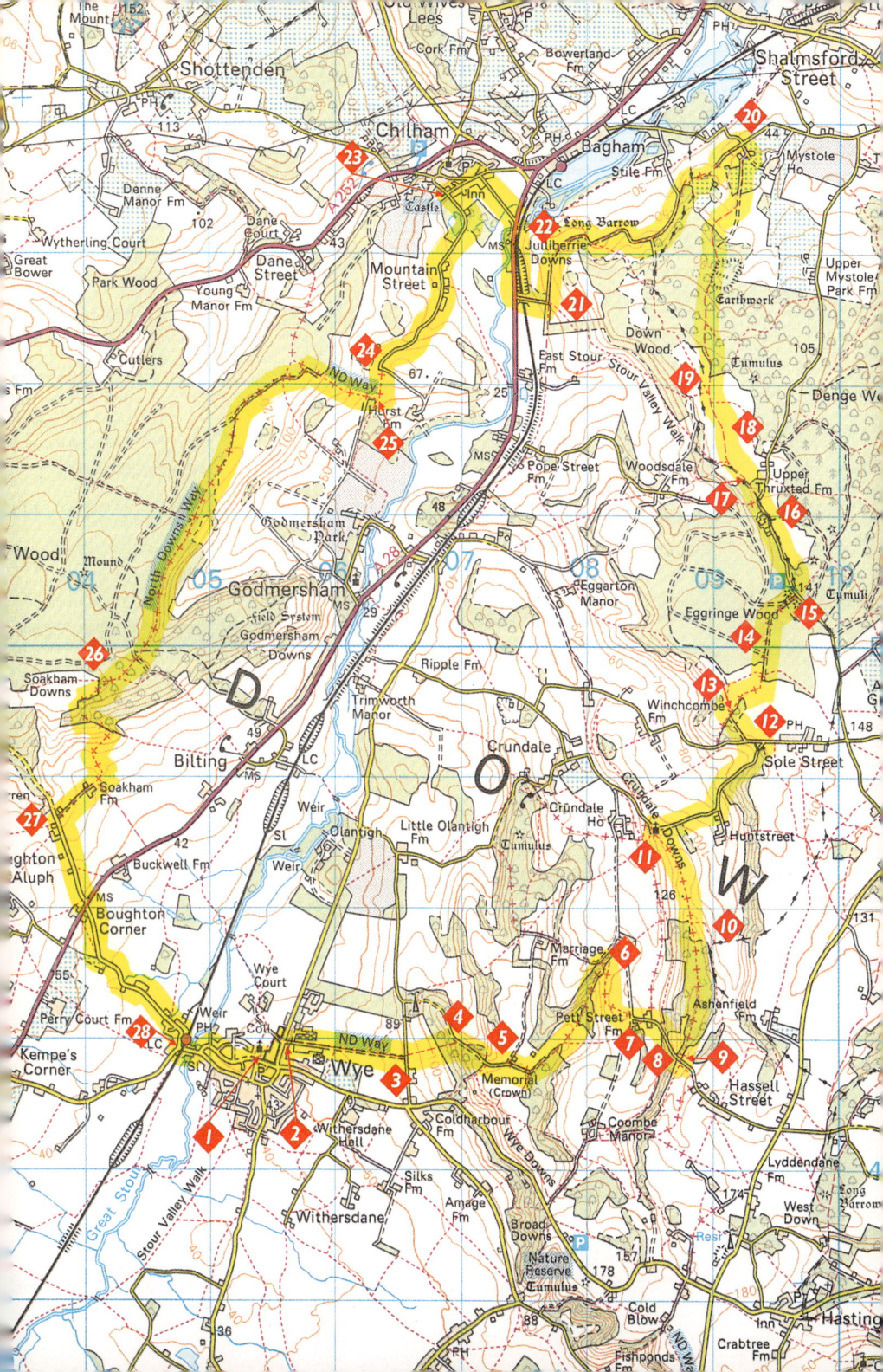

On the North Downs above the Elham Valley, north of Folkestone

A short, easy ride on top of the eastern end of the North Downs near Folkestone starts with a climb through woodland and alternates quiet lanes with off-road sections throughout its length. The route could easily be linked to route 10, by leaving at instruction 6 and joining the other route at Alkham or Ewell Minnis.

Warning

There are two sections on this route which are prone to get muddy, between instructions 9 & 10 and between 11 & 12. Be prepared to find road alternatives

Refreshments

*Endeavour PH, **Wootton**
Kings Arms PH, **Elham**
Jackdaw PH, **Denton**
Otherwise, make detour to
Swingfield Street or **Densole***

Start

The Endeavour PH, Wootton, 8 miles north of Folkestone, just off the A260

P You may park in the pub car park **only** if you are going to use the pub. Please do not abuse this. There is limited car parking near the village hall in Wootton. Otherwise park your car in Densole and join the route at instruction 10, or in Elham and join the route at instruction 17 at Rakeshole Farm

Distance and grade

12 miles

Easy/moderate

Terrain

The ride is on top of the Downs so there are no major climbs. The steepest is the last one back up the hill to Wootton

Nearest railway

Shepherdswell, 3 miles northeast of Wootton

Wootton

St Johns Farm

Boyington Court

Densole

The Butterfly Centre, Swingfield (8)

A large greenhouse contains an exhibition explaining the life-cycle of butterflies. There is also an area for British butterflies, a landscaped garden and many tropical plants.

Reindeer Wood near Densole

Paddlesworth

Shuttlesfield

Acrise Place

Rakeshole Farm

Tappington Hall

1 With your back to the pub R 'Geddinge, Shepherdswell'

2 At the bottom of the hill opposite a sign for Eythorne and Shepperdswell on your left R onto track through woodland

3 At concrete track by barn bear R

4 At T-j with road L 'Selsted ¾, Lydden 4, Folkestone 6'

5 At T-j L 'Swingfield, Lydden, Dover'

6 At next T-j R 'Swingfield 1, Folkestone 6'

7 Shortly after a left turning to Swingfield Street, on RH bend, bear L (in effect SA) (NS)

8 After sharp RH bend by houses, just before mast L onto track. Horseshoe sign

9 Continue in same direction, ignoring turnings and crossing several X-roads at right angles until reaching A260 (the last section may be muddy, in which case turn R off track to join A260, which runs parallel)

10 At T-j with A260 L, then 1st R just after sign for Hawkinge onto Pay Street

11 After ½ mile, opposite 1st turning on right L onto track

12 This is muddy at the end. Join tarmac. At X-roads with road R, then 1st R just after Cat and Custard Pot PH 'Acrise, Swingfield'

13 After 100 yards leave tarmac and turn L across field beneath telephone lines. At the edge of field with gate ahead turn L on track between hedge and fence. Pass underneath telephone lines aiming towards farm and gate at far end of field

14 At road R following signs for Acrise

15 At T-j R 'Acrise, Swingfield', then 1st L by triangle of grass 'Swingfield, Lydden'

16 At bottom of hill, on sharp RH bend, L 'Ladwood, Henbury'

17 At T-j SA 'Rakeshole Farm'

18 From tarmac to track to earth to track and back to tarmac. At road R

19 At A260 L 'Canterbury', then 1st R 'Wootton' to return to start

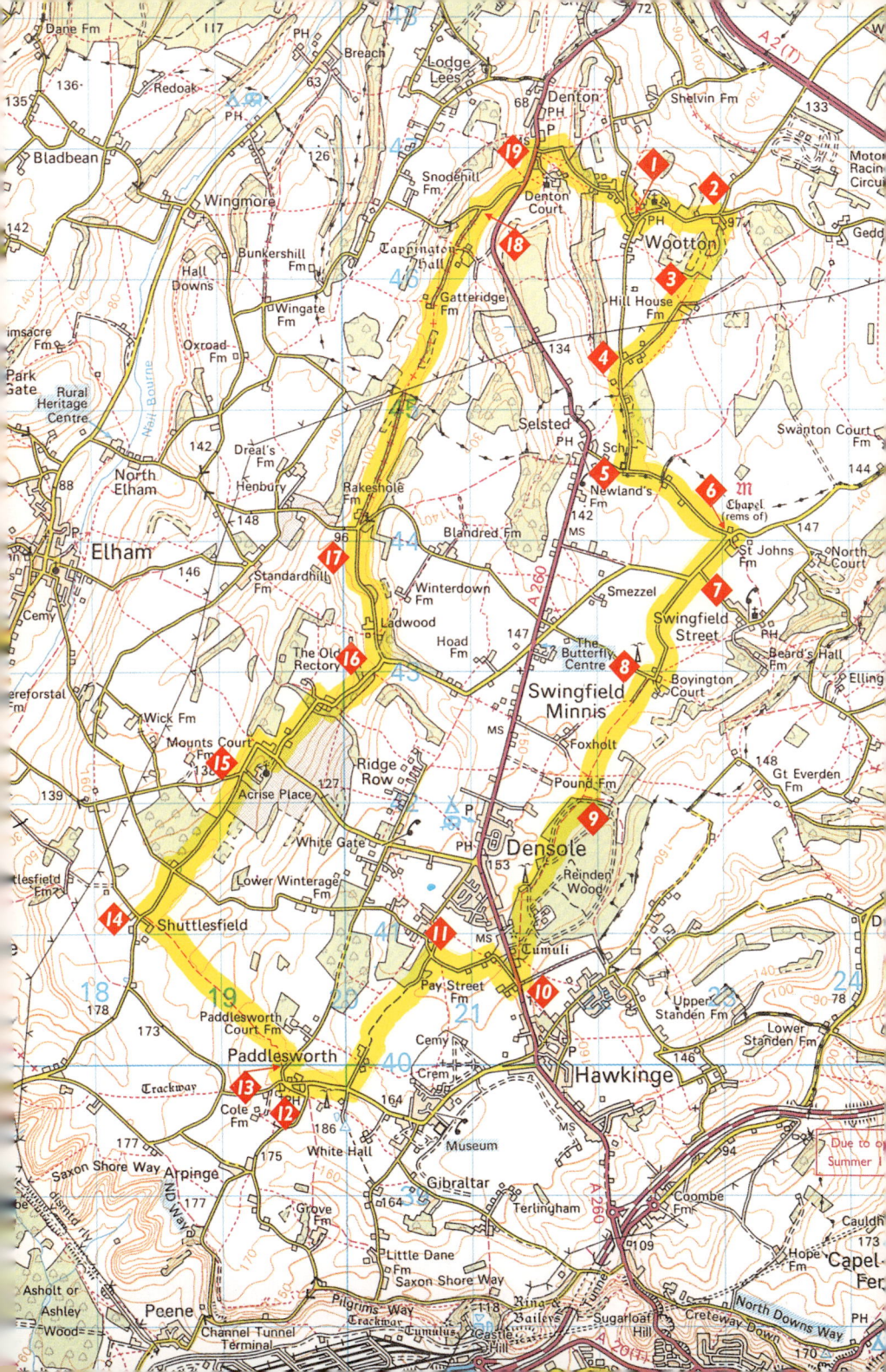

Start

The Old Gaol in the centre of Dover

 P Follow signs

 Distance and grade

16 miles

 Moderate

Terrain

Three climbs, one of 400 feet from Dover to the A2, one of 330 feet from Temple Ewell to Ewell Minnis and the last from Alkham to the top of the Downs

 Nearest railway

Dover

10 *Behind the White Cliffs: the North Downs near Dover*

Starting from the centre of Dover, the ride climbs steeply via the North Downs Way, crossing the A2 as it continues northwards along leafy tracks. The route swings south into and out of the steep valley in which Dover is situated. A stiff challenge faces the fit and those who are determined not to get off on the climb up from Kearnsey to Ewell Minnis. A pub awaits you in Ewell Minnis if you need sustenance. Through Alkham and a steep climb on the road leaves you at the top of the Downs, with a long descent along farm tracks then through an industrial estate to return to Dover.

 Refreshments

Lots of choice in **Dover**
Fox PH, **Temple Ewell**
New Castle Inn, **Ewell Minnis**
Marquis of Granby PH, **Alkham**

Dover   Connaught Park   A2   Pineham   Napchester   Temple Farm   Temple Ewell   Kearsney

Dover Castle (1)

Dover Castle is one of the largest and best preserved castles in England and has the longest recorded history of any fortress in England. It is thought to have been part of an Iron Age hill fort and there are Roman, medieval, Georgian and Victorian remains. In the grounds is the Roman lighthouse, the Pharos, the tallest surviving roman structure in Britain. The keep, curtain walls and outer fortifications were built in the 12th century and it was strengthened again in the 13th. It was changed greatly during the Napoleonic Wars when many of the towers had their tops cut off to provide artillery platforms. Most of the castle is open to the public and there are excellent views over the English Channel from the battlements. The secret tunnels and war headquarters of Vice-Admiral Ramsay can be toured at Hellfire Corner.

The White Cliffs Experience and the Dover Museum

This 'museum' brings the history of Dover alive with audio-visual shows, talking exhibits and even an old ferry deck that can make you feel sea sick. Next door is the Dover Museum which houses original artefacts from prehistoric times up to the present day.

Dover Old Town Gaol

Audio-visual techniques take you back to Victorian times to hear the stories of the prisoners and gaolers. The courtroom, cells, exercise yard and bathroom have been reconstructed.

Bushy Ruff

Ewell Minnis

Alkham

Poulton Farm

Hospital

1 From the Old Gaol R on Ladywell. At traffic lights diagonally L onto Park Avenue

2 At T-j with Connaught Road L, then just before T-j with Barton Road R by the Primary School up Old Charlton Road

3 Just past St Edmunds Catholic School on your left, L onto Roman Road 'North Downs Way'

4 At fork at end of tarmac R 'Byway. North Downs Way'. When you reach the busy A2, keep following the North Downs Way.

5 At road L (in effect SA). Just after passing triangle of grass, with no through road by a white house on your right, R onto track 'Byway'

6 At next road SA 'Byway' across field towards wood then bear R along edge of wood. Follow in same direction to road

7 At road L, following signs for Whitfield

8 At X-roads with A256 SA onto Nursery Lane

9 At T-j with Singledge Lane R 'Shepherdswell, Coldred'

10 Shortly after Longfield Farm and caravan park on your right next left on no through road 'Public Bridleway'

11 L on track before farm, following main track over field, under A2 and immediately L through double metal gates to gate in far left hand corner of field (may be rough/muddy)

12 From gate bear R down through field towards wood and

red-brick houses in the valley

13 Good descent to road. At road SA 'Alkham 3. To the church'

14 Under railway bridge. At T-j with Alkham Road (B2060) R, then immediately R on tarmac 'Bridleway'

15 Tough challenge to cycle up this hill! Follow tarmac/track/single track in same direction (may be rough/muddy). At edge of wood follow RH field edge to next blue arrow on white sign

16 Follow for almost 1 mile. Take 1st tarmac lane on L by house. Past New Castle Inn. At T-j with road by telephone box L then R 'Public Bridleway'

17 Through wood, across field. At road R then L 'Hougham 2, Capel 2½'

18 Steep climb. At X-roads L 'St Radigund's 1¾, River 2½'

19 On sharp LH bend by barns R (in effect SA) onto track

20 Through farm, down road past industrial estate. At roundabout SA onto Coombe Valley Road

21 At X-roads with main road R, following one-way system and signs for town centre (follow Cherry Tree Avenue, Barton Road, Frith Road, Charlton Green Road), then opposite Job Centre get into RH lane and follow signs for police station to return to the start

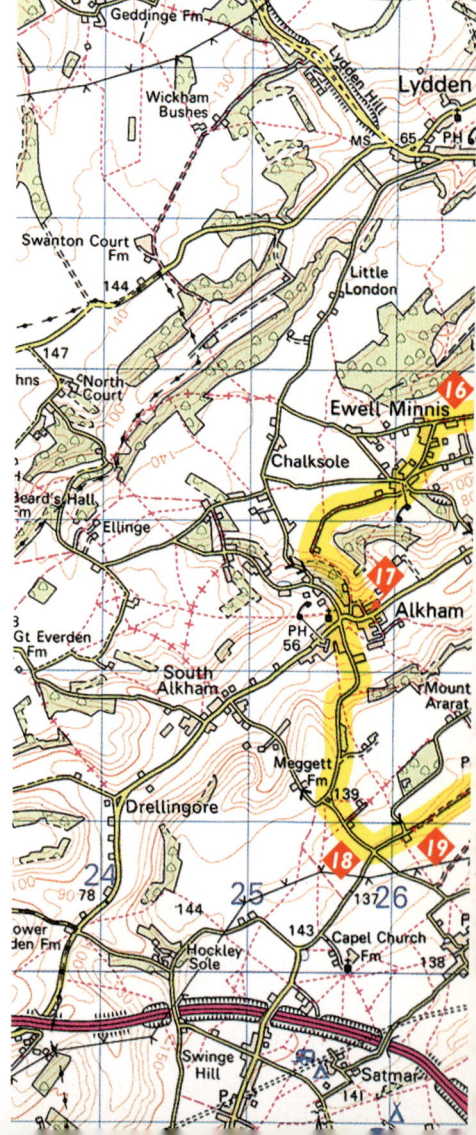

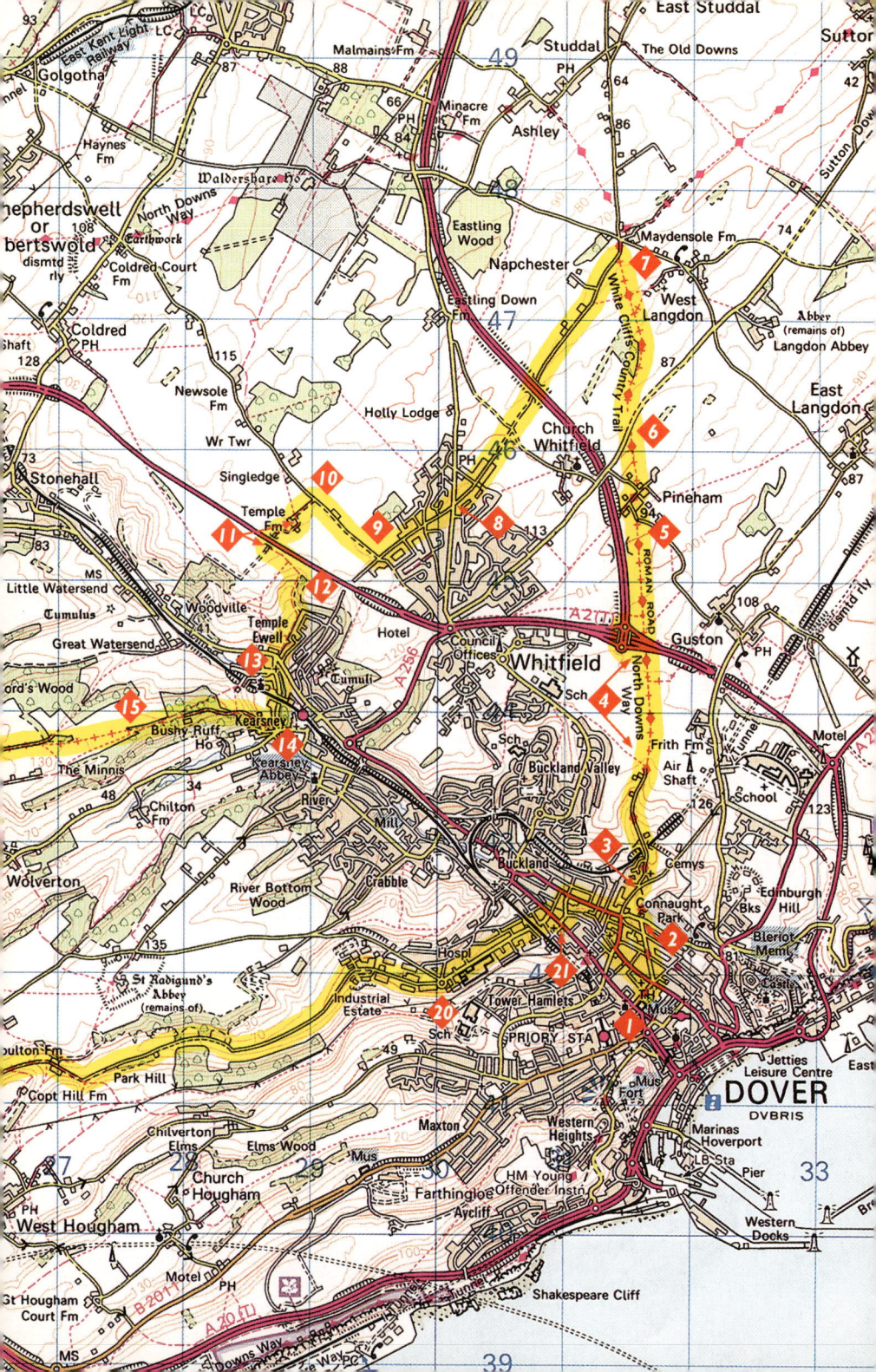

Cycle Cycle Cycle
TOURS TOURS TOURS

The Ordnance Survey Cycle Tours series

os Ordnance Survey

Cycle

21 one-day routes in
**East Anglia
North**

TOURS

Nick Cotton

- ◆ Around Birmingham
- ◆ Around London
- ◆ Avon, Somerset & Wiltshire
- ◆ Berks, Bucks & Oxfordshire
- ◆ Central Scotland
- ◆ Cornwall & Devon
- ◆ Cumbria & the Lakes
- ◆ Dorset, Hampshire & Isle of Wight
- ◆ East Anglia – North
- ◆ East Anglia – South
- ◆ Gloucestershire & Hereford & Worcester
- ◆ Kent, Surrey & Sussex
- ◆ North Wales & The Marches
- ◆ North Yorkshire & Teesside
- ◆ Northumberland & County Durham
- ◆ Peak District
- ◆ Southern Scotland
- ◆ South, West & Mid-Wales
- ◆ Yorkshire Dales

*T*he whole series is available from all good bookshops or by mail order direct from the publisher (postage and packing £2 per order). Payment can be made by credit card or cheque/postal order in the following ways:

By phone Phone your order through on our special *Credit Card Hotline* on *01933 443863 (Fax: 01933 443849)*. Speak to our customer service team during office hours (9am to 5pm) or leave a message on the answer machine, quoting your full credit card number plus expiry date and your full name and address and reference.

By post Simply fill out the order form (you may photocopy it) and send it to: *Philip's Direct, 27 Sanders Road, Wellingborough, Northants NN8 4NL.*

Ordnance Survey Cycle TOURS ORDER FORM

I wish to order the following titles	Quantity @ £9.99 each	£ Total
AROUND BIRMINGHAM	☐ 0 600 58623 5 ➤	
AROUND LONDON	☐ 0 600 58845 9 ➤	
AVON, SOMERSET & WILTSHIRE	☐ 0 600 58664 2 ➤	
BERKS, BUCKS & OXFORDSHIRE	☐ 0 600 58156 X ➤	
CENTRAL SCOTLAND	☐ 0 600 59005 4 ➤	
CORNWALL & DEVON	☐ 0 600 58124 1 ➤	
CUMBRIA & THE LAKES	☐ 0 600 58126 8 ➤	
DORSET, HAMPSHIRE & ISLE OF WIGHT	☐ 0 600 58667 7 ➤	
EAST ANGLIA – NORTH	☐ 0 600 59219 7 ➤	
EAST ANGLIA – SOUTH	☐ 0 600 58125 X ➤	
GLOUCESTERSHIRE & HEREFORD & WORCESTER	☐ 0 600 58665 0 ➤	
KENT, SURREY & SUSSEX	☐ 0 600 58666 9 ➤	
NORTH WALES & THE MARCHES	☐ 0 600 59007 0 ➤	
NORTH YORKSHIRE & TEESSIDE	☐ 0 600 59103 4 ➤	
NORTHUMBERLAND & COUNTY DURHAM	☐ 0 600 59105 0 ➤	
PEAK DISTRICT	☐ 0 600 58889 0 ➤	
SOUTHERN SCOTLAND	☐ 0 600 58624 3 ➤	
SOUTH, WEST & MID-WALES	☐ 0 600 58846 7 ➤	
YORKSHIRE DALES	☐ 0 600 58847 5 ➤	

Name..

Address...

....

....Postcode........................

◆ **Add £2 postage and packing per order**

◆ All available titles will normally be dispatched within 5 working days of receipt of order but please allow up to 28 days for delivery

◆ Whilst every effort is made to keep prices low, the publisher reserves the right to increase prices at short notice

☐ Please tick this box if you do not wish your name to be used by other carefully selected organisations that may wish to send you information about other products and services

Registered Office: 2-4 Heron Quays, London E14 4JP
Registered in England number: 3597451

Total price of order £ ☐

(including postage and packing at £2 per order)

I enclose a cheque/postal order, for £ ☐

made payable to *Octopus Publishing Group Ltd*,

or please debit my ☐ Mastercard ☐ American Express

☐ Visa account by £ ☐

Account no

☐☐☐☐ ☐☐☐☐ ☐☐☐☐ ☐☐☐☐

Expiry date ☐☐ ☐☐

Signature...

Post to: Philip's Direct, 27 Sanders Road, Wellingborough, Northants NN8 4NL